P9-ARD-466

Latinnovating™

Green American Jobs
and the Latinos Creating Them

By Graciela Tiscareño-Sato

Gracefully Global Group

Gracefully Global Group LLC
Hayward, California
www.gracefullyglobal.com

© 2011, Gracefully Global Group, LLC. All rights reserved.

No part of this book may be reproduced, stored in a retrieval system, or transmitted by any other means without the written permission of the author.

ISBN: 978-0-9834760-0-9

Library of Congress Control Number: 2011924447

Printed in the United States of America. This book is printed with soy inks on acid-free paper that is FSC Certified. Produced by THRIVE Publishing™, San Francisco CA www.thrivebooks.com

Mixed Sources
Product group from well-managed
forests and other controlled sources

Cert no. SW-COC-002283
www.fsc.org
© 1996 Forest Stewardship Council

URL Disclaimer
All the Internet addresses given in this book were valid at the time of going to press. However, due to the dynamic nature of the Internet, some addresses may have changed or sites may have changed or ceased to exist since publication. While the author and publisher regret any inconvenience this may cause readers, no responsibility for any such changes can be accepted by either the author or the publisher.

I dedicate this book to:

My over-the-top, eco-conscious children:
Milagro — "The opposite of trash is recycling."
Kotomi — "I can make a dress for my doll with that old sock!"
Kiyoshi — "That moldy tomato goes in the food recycling."

For you and for your descendants, we strive for a healthier planet.

My husband Genro Sato: for making my irregular "writing nights" possible, enjoying time with our children so I could go somewhere quiet to create something to inform and inspire others.

My parents Arturo and Tina Tiscareño: who taught me to *always* embrace and celebrate my Mexican heritage and the Spanish language, while aspiring to achieve more in life.

Praise for *Latinnovating*

"*Latinnovating* provides rich insight into the exciting possibilities and opportunities that exist within the green economy. Graciela Tiscareño-Sato does an outstanding job of chronicling how Latino entrepreneurs are positioning themselves today as leaders across different industries. These stories of success and sustainability will inspire readers and serve as a valuable tool for all those working to build a cleaner, greener future."
　　　—*Phaedra Ellis-Lamkins, Chief Executive Officer, Green For All*

"*Latinnovating* gives an inspiring look into how Latinos across the country are transforming the business world to be friendlier to our environment and long-term sustainability. This book is a valuable read for business owners, activists, and young people looking to join the growing green economy."
　　　—*Adrianna Quintero, Director of Latino Outreach,*
　　　Natural Resources Defense Council

"For many years, the Latino entrepreneurial spirit has quietly powered America's economy. At last, a book has been published that brings these hidden stories of economic contribution out of the darkness. In producing *Latinnovating*, Graciela shines a bright spotlight on Latino entrepreneurs innovating new solutions and playing significant roles in the green economy. Simultaneously, these stories of highly educated Latinos demonstrate the urgent need to improve Latino high school and college graduation rates so that many more environmental entrepreneurs will burst onto the scene to power America through the 21st century."
　　　—*Aida Alvarez, Chair, Latino Community Foundation and former*
　　　Administrator of the U.S. Small Business Administration

"Finally a book has been written that brings to life the inspiring stories of entrepreneurs building businesses in the right-thing-to-do, yet hard-to-monetize green economy. The stories in this book captivated me. You will quickly realize these are not only stories about the green movement and Latino entrepreneurs, but also of the will of the human spirit to innovate and create. As a Latino, this collection of stories is particularly special to me."
—*Marcos J. Cordero, LEED AP and CEO, Green Business Bureau*

"Graciela highlights incredible success stories of Latino leaders not only participating in but creating business opportunities in the green economy. These stories are a true source for inspiration for young people and for professionals in transition. As Hispanic-owned businesses play an increasingly important role as engines driving economic recovery, *Latinnovating* shows how this community is also making a difference towards a better planet. Given the international connections that Hispanic businesses have, they are the latent force that can transform how business is done in the Americas to improve the quality of the environment on a large scale. This book is a must-read for any business wanting to take advantage of green opportunities and for those looking for green entry points."
—*Magda Cardenas, Director of Marketing and Communications, Greater Washington D.C. Hispanic Chamber of Commerce*

"Graciela Tiscareño-Sato writes with a passion for the environment and Latino issues that is unmatched. I enthusiastically recommend her book, *Latinnovating.* Anyone interested in a green career will find the book to be an invaluable resource. Young Latinos interested in a green career will find the book and its many stories of Latino success to be particularly inspirational."
—*Bruce Matzner, Managing Partner, Diversity and Recruitment Solutions*

"In the midst of a landscape of public opinion that is saturated with weeds—that is, negative stereotypes about Hispanics—this book offers instead radiant flowers: the positive, creative, brilliant and extraordinary contributions that Latinos are making for the

"These powerful stories will make a huge impact on many Latinos who today are in the same situation these leaders once were. As educators we need to share these unique and important stories with the young people we serve."
— *Héctor M. González, College and Career Coach, John Hancock High School, Chicago Illinois*

"I was moved to tears as I read the story of Frank Ramirez. The story of his youth is unfortunately very familiar to me. As an Academic Advisor at a state community college, I hear young and not-so-young Latinos relaying similar stories. I was so inspired by Frank's story because I believe when fate intervenes it is purposeful. I wish there were more individuals who could see Latinos for their potential and not get blinded by good intentions. The world needs more stories of perseverance like that of Mr. Ramirez and the others in the pages of *Latinnovating*. Parents should read this book to help their child see the big picture and create a bigger vision for their lives. High school and college students will gain an understanding of how others before them have found success through education. They will see that they can make a difference in the world. Lastly, counselors and advisors should read this book to gain understanding of how to put students on the path of self knowledge and life-long learning no matter what their current situation happens to be."
— *Marla Manchego, Single Parent Counselor, Advising, Career, and Counseling Center, Front Range Community College*

"As a high school student, this book provided me something I had not seen before—role models that look like me. Through higher education and honoring their cultural values, these ten innovators are contributing to the American economy in very significant ways. This has excited me about the possibilities that lie ahead. I now know what to do to emulate these inspirational leaders. If you're the parent of a teenager or college student, this book makes an excellent gift for the information and actionable inspiration it provides to those of us mapping out our professional futures."
— *Kevin Iglesias, Student and Congressional Hispanic Caucus Institute Ready to Lead Program Participant, Wheaton High School, Maryland*

"At a time when many in our world are focusing on sustainability and on "going green," Graciela tells you the stories of Latino innovators from a culture that has always practiced these values. These business men and women have created successful companies and are committed to environmental entrepreneurship. This book is definitely a one of a kind and a true inspiration to young Latinos everywhere. High school and college students will especially enjoy the personal stories and the paths of success that these leaders have taken in life."
—*Kimberly Herrera, Coordinator, Student Activities,*
Anne Arundel Community College

"As American Latinos, our emphasis in life normally lies with job, car, home, family–the American Dream but with family added to the equation. Green Education? Sadly enough, this hasn't yet become part of our national psyche. As a Hayward City Councilman who is very much into educating our youth–Latino and otherwise–and greening our City, I am most impressed with *Latinnovating*, as it touches on both areas. An extended American Dream come true—job, car, home, family, education and green! *¡Ya era hora! ¡Dale gas, Graciela!*"
—*José Francisco Zermeño Cárdenas, City of Hayward Councilman*
and Professor of Spanish, Chabot College

"Some of today's most innovative business leaders began their lives as economically-disadvantaged children from strong Hispanic families. These families, rooted in their faith for a better future and a propensity to conserve and reuse, raised creative problem solvers and critical thinkers. Equipped with higher education credentials and a lifetime of learning, these same people are now helping to move our nation towards a more sustainable future by causing changes in our unsustainable industrial status quo. Graciela weaves their personal stories, educational paths, industry insights and actionable resources for today's students and job seekers into a truly unique tapestry. This book delivers powerful messages and paths to emulate that will surely inspire the next generation of environmental entrepreneurs to succeed despite their current circumstances. *¡Adelante Graciela!*"
—*Victor Arias Jr., Senior Client Partner, Korn/Ferry International*

"Realism is a difficult term to encompass in our lives, but that is exactly what we need and find in *Latinnovating*. Through the depiction of personal stories and first-hand experiences of Latinos facilitating the green movement, you'll be moved by their efforts to improve energy efficiency and optimize the use of natural resources. I emphatically recommend this book to anyone who needs a green awakening. Graciela does an amazing job of creating a realistic awareness of the environmental habits that are saving our planet today!"
— *Iliah Pérez, Marketing & Business Development/Director at Large,*
Contra Costa Hispanic Chamber of Commerce

Praise for the Live Presentation of *Latinnovating*

"Graciela is amazing, motivating and real. In fact, as a keynote speaker for Business Leadership Week at Texas State University, she highlighted the stories of Carmen, Frank, Luis and Rosamaria living their lives filled with curiosity and passion (just like Graciela). The students and professors were spellbound by the stories of these pioneers."
—*Janet Riola Hale, JD, Senior Lecturer and Sponsor of Net Impact*
Student Organization, Department of Finance and Economics,
Texas State University-San Marcos

"You were exactly what we were hoping for in a distinguished lecturer and what you shared with the students exceeded our expectations! I know the students learned a lot of valuable lessons through your interactive presentation and remarkable stories about sustainable businesses started by Latinos. It was very special to have you speak about your book, the Latino community and what a difference these business owners have made in our world. It is an area of business that should get much more attention. I am glad you could come speak to the students and our community to help open many eyes to something new and exciting."
—*Arin Ely, Student Development Coordinator & Academic Advisor*
McCoy College of Business Administration,
Texas State University-San Marcos

Table of Contents

Acknowledgments

To Bruce Matzner for asking me to write the feature article for the fall issue of *Hispanic MBA Magazine*. In asking me what ideas I had for the article and in listening to the questions I had in mind ("As the green economy takes shape, what role, if any, is the Latino business community playing?. . ."), this book was ultimately born.

To Mitch Posada for generously sharing your network of people working toward a more sustainable economy. Thank you for introducing me to several people in this book who then led me to others.

To our German au pairs Linda, Mandy, Jasmin and Nansin: you were each instrumental parts of my support village, playing with my children, transporting them, feeding them and loving them so that I could be at peace to work and to write this book a few hours at a time. I couldn't have done it without you!

To Julia Hubbel for guiding me during my transition from military officer to civilian in the late '90s. Thank you for teaching me that principled networking means giving first, receiving second. I have applied your lessons many times and will always do so.

To my fellow author and friend Frank Carbajal for asking me to partner with you to create the Silicon Valley Latino Leadership Summit immediately after we witnessed the deeply disappointing CNN *Latino in America* series. Thank you for choosing action over complaining and for including me in the endeavor. We've created a unique leadership summit to move the dial forward for the next ten years. A special thank you for igniting the spark I needed to get this book done when it was languishing behind my two other manuscripts. Thanks for helping me get my priorities straight! Thank you for offering me the forum to introduce this book to our combined networks of amazing people.

To all my interviewees, the *Latinnovators*—Frank, Carmen, Rodrigo, Humberto, Sandra, Monica, Dennis, Rosamaria, Robert and Luis: thank you for your time and for trusting me with pieces of your extraordinary lives. After every interview I asked myself, "How am I going to write about that phenomenal set of events and successes? Will I be able to do this story justice?" You're truly the inspiration our nation's students need. I'm committed to ensuring as many as possible hear about, and hopefully emulate, your accomplishments, innovations and wisdom.

To Ann Matranga, my friend and developmental editor, who provided the just-in-time advice I needed but had been avoiding that really made a difference.

To the very talented THRIVE Publishing™ team, you're exactly who I needed to bring this book into the light, starting with publisher Caterina Rando, who brought her high energy and visionary excellence to this project, and including Tammy Tribble, Ruth Schwartz and Karen Gargiulo.

To Tammy Tribble, graphic designer extraordinaire—thanks for your truly awesome design and for speaking up with "I work for a publisher in San Francisco," at that birthday party. This classic mommy/Girl Scout networking led me to Caterina and THRIVE Publishing™! Thanks for enduring all my creative energy and questions during the cover design process.

To Ruth Schwartz, for your wisdom, patience and mentoring.

To my editor, Karen Gargiulo, for masterfully cutting ten percent of my manuscript without losing a single bit of substance. That's magic.

To my parents Arturo and Tina Tiscareño: *Les debo todo. Les debo el orgullo de ser Mexicana, les debo la habilidad de hablar mi querido idioma, español, porque insistieron que lo habláramos en casa durante mi niñez. Les debo el deseo de recibir más y más educación, y siempre querer saber más de todo. Les debo todo porque ustedes hicieron la decisión de venir a este país que nos ha dado todas las oportunidades para salir adelante y obtener una vida feliz y exitosa. ¡Espero y estén muy orgullosos porque hice este proyecto para documentar las historias de varios Latinos súper exitosos!*

To my children, Milagro, Kotomi and Kiyoshi my trilogy of love and goofiness. It is to you that we owe a cleaner planet, with cleaner air and water, so that you can enjoy this blue Earth with your own children and grandchildren someday. We cannot irreparably damage this world and leave you to explain to your children why their ancestors ruined it—that's not an option. For you I write this book, so that as adults you will know that your mother cared deeply about our planet, about our culture, about higher education and the doors it opens, and about personal and professional achievement. I give to you also my example as an entrepreneur and permission to create your own businesses based on your own creativity, passion and ideas. Above all, you know I always found a way to work flexibly, to be always near you in your youngest years. I was never going to be a mommy regretting that I missed your childhood. This is why I chose to write this first book while you were young; so that you could watch me create something important over a long period of time. I wanted you to appreciate the tenacity, work and dedication it takes to be an author. I wanted us to be together during the process so that one day you may wish to write something deeply important to you. I wanted my choices, my writing, my passion and my discipline to serve as an example to all of you, to reinforce what I tell you every day: You are highly creative. You are extraordinarily intelligent. You are great readers, thinkers and problem solvers. You are loving and giving people. You have so much to offer the world. You are leaders. You will inspire and positively impact many people in your lives. I adore and cherish each of you, my sweeties.

To my husband Genro: you are my lifelong love and partner in all facets of everything that matters. Dating back to those innocent yet challenging college days of our senior year in Berkeley, when we took on the responsibility of running the Cal marching band together, I cannot think of anything I've ever accomplished that didn't include your direct involvement. You're my sounding board, my business partner, my reviewer, my web guru, my network administrator, my first editor and so much more. You're the one who asks great questions and the one who sits me down to relax, watch some sci-fi channel and drink some wine when my brain really needs a break. You're the most competent and loving father that exists, hands down—no contest. We survived nearly a decade of my military deployments and their unique challenges, a transition out of the military into civilian life, an interstate move, the birth of a severely premature baby and her 137-day hospitalization, medical challenges, insurance challenges, her blindness, the birth of two other beautiful healthy children, special education advocacy challenges and through it all, we've shined and succeeded together. As I have often asked myself—and will do so for the rest of my life—I wonder what I did to deserve you, my love. Thank you for being next to me through it all.

Special Thanks
To Our Earliest Supporters

Kathy Heilmann

Elena Velez

Manuel Noda

Agustina Tiscareño

Johnny Velasquez

Angela De Jesus

Martha Hernandez

Gina Vanderhorst

Nansin Akar

Marta Layseca

Eileen Taveras

Melanie Smith

Sonya Sigler

Sal Amin

Christina Cuyler

PJ Stafford

Justine Cromer

Ann Matranga

Ivonne Laura Thompson

Anabel Granados

Jaron Nemes

Pedro Kanof

Mimi Hernandez

Marcos Cordero

Claudia Romero

Melinda Berumen

Janet Hale

Dr. William T. and
Mrs. Deborah A. Chittenden

Laura Edwards

Dr. John Falvey

Andre Hill

Peggy Montano

Luis Peña

Reina Duarte

Humberto Rincon

Marla Manchego

Janyce Harper

Alba Gonzalez-Nylander

Frank Ramirez

Edgar Mejia

Gina Miranda

Lorenzo Gonzales

Dennis Salazar

Monica DeZulueta

Ben Tiscareño

Federico Subervi, PhD

National Hispanic
Environmental Council

Introduction

Latinnovating
(Lah-TEE-no-vay-ting)

Definition:

• Industrial and social innovation rooted in and influenced by Latino culture

• Based on familial values of creative reuse, preservation and conservation of resources

Objective:
Those who are *latinnovating* work to improve processes, products and boost energy efficiencies to support our modern lifestyle. They create economic opportunity and prosperity for their families, communities and our nation. It's *not* about self deprevation.

*A*s I wrapped up the first set of interviews with American Latino innovators running sustainable businesses, CNN® began to promote its "groundbreaking series," *Latino in America*, anchored by Soledad O'Brien.

I wondered how many educated, professional Latinos—like the people I had interviewed—would be included in four hours of CNN coverage. Like millions of others across North America and Mexico, I watched the two-part series and was profoundly disappointed. The only successful Latinos included in the series were television celebrities. Everyone else was a real-life stereotype: the struggling, just-arrived immigrant who speaks English with a strong accent and repeatedly fails the exam to become a law enforcement officer; the teenage girl who is unexpectedly pregnant; the suicidal teen Latina; the Latina student with many siblings who is failing junior high school because her mother expects her to miss school to provide child care. I realized that my agenda and CNN's were very different.

Why was CNN perpetuating stereotypes? Did Soledad O'Brien and the CNN production staff not know or have access to educated Latinos in leadership roles in business and academia? Where were the college-educated professionals, the people with advanced degrees in business, the entrepreneurs, the college professors, the American Latino success stories, the Latinos who create jobs and opportunities for all Americans? I posted my reaction on the *Latino in America* Facebook® fan page: "Soledad, Soledad . . . you let me down hard, Soledad."

In the spring of 2009, I worked for a German software communications company. I led a team that was creating a key component of the company's global sustainability initiatives. I learned about units of carbon emissions, energy efficiency certificates, megawatts, gigawatts, and many other terms and concepts of energy efficiency. I developed a program with an energy company to audit our customers' data centers so we could showcase the economic savings and carbon emissions reductions that accompanied our newest solutions. I was fully absorbed in the world of corporate sustainability initiatives.

During this time, Bruce Matzner, publisher of several magazines including one for the National Society of Hispanic MBAs (NSHMBA), asked me to write a feature article for the Society's conference issue. He asked me to pitch some ideas to him. I shared with him the intriguing questions that had been brewing in my mind:

As the American green economy picks up momentum, what role, if any, is the Latino business community playing? Are we participating in ways that are not well-known by the general public? Are we excluded from the action? Does America's fastest growing minority group know or care much about the environmental movement and sustainable businesses? Is anyone communicating with the Latino community to encourage sustainable choices now, and in future decades? Do Latinos believe that climate change is real and that remedies are needed? How is this country reinventing itself along with its economic infrastructure? Who is making it happen?

Bruce encouraged me to pursue these questions. As I reached out to fellow members of NSHMBA to identify innovators and business leaders in the green movement, the names started rolling in. I put together a questionnaire. Each interview with an innovator led me to several others. I interviewed a dozen people, then wrote, researched and published the article titled, *"The Greening of America: Hispanic Environmental Advocates Take the Lead."* Due to the space constraints of a magazine article, I barely summarized the significant contributions each person was making in the green economy. Readers reacted positively—they wanted to know more about the entrepreneurs and leaders discussed in the article.

When the disappointing CNN series aired the same month my article was published, it occurred to me that there was a certain synchronicity in the timing. It was then that I decided to write a book with a point of view far different than CNN's Ms. O'Brien: to reveal Latino-led innovation and entrepreneurial leadership within the emerging green economy. My themes included sustainability as a foundation for 21st century survival and growth, the bedrock importance of education and the powerful entrepreneurial spunk of Latinos that is benefiting all Americans. These are just the first ten stories. There will be many more.

I sent copies of the published magazine article to my interviewees and told them I was going to turn their stories into a book. I expanded my initial questionnaire and interviewed most of them again. I found additional entrepreneurs in different industries to give the book a broader scope. Twenty-two interview sessions and hundreds of solitary research and writing hours later, I saw that the American Latino community is not just watching the action; we are significant actors in innovation. I became acutely aware that our contributions have, so far, escaped the mainstream media. Instead, mainstream America only sees images of Latinos in stories about poverty, deportation, violence at the border and undocumented nannies—the stereotypes reinforced by CNN. Americans have no idea how deeply the Latino community cares about environmental issues. They have no idea we're actively engaged in action.

We are creating technologies that will immediately reduce energy consumption based on dirty fossil fuels. We are creating social justice programs to ensure that disenfranchised communities enjoy the benefits of this new economy. We are reinventing entire industries. Some of us are turning our backs on the status quo to launch our own sustainable businesses. We are demonstrating that businesses built for sustainability are indeed successful. I uncovered dramatic examples of leadership across a variety of sectors in our new, greener economy.

There are forces at play to reduce our national carbon footprint, to slowly begin to wean us from foreign oil, to reduce landfill-bound waste and to create and harness alternative energy sources. The green economy is more important than most Americans realize. It is an economic and industrial transformation that will change every detail of national and daily life. The green economy is to 21st century America what the railroad was to 19th century America. After the rails were laid, *everything* changed.

Why are Latinos intricately involved in this move toward sustainable practices? I believe we are honoring long-standing and deeply embedded cultural values of conservation, preservation of natural resources and creative reuse. As a communicator, I wanted to re-present successful, educated Latinos who were born in the United States or who came here as young children and surpassed their parents' dreams. Several of my interviewees were born into a life of extreme scarcity—some were not. Creative reuse was necessary for survival, as you will see in several stories. These future leaders were rooted in culturally-driven environmentalism as children because their ancestors knew preservation of our world was critical. All of the people you will read about in this book hungered for more from life. Through intervention and encouragement, each of them achieved their own version of the American dream through education. I am one of them.

I am the oldest of five U.S.-born children of Mexican immigrants who arrived here in the mid-1960s. Socio-economically speaking, we never reached anything beyond the lower-middle class. My parents purchased a modest home, held jobs in and out of the home, paid taxes and prepared other people's taxes. They eventually started their own tailoring business during my father's so-called retirement, and grew it steadily for fourteen years. They now enjoy real retirement, traveling around the western United States and Mexico in their RV. They achieved their American dream.

My parents insisted we all speak Spanish at home, ignoring us if we spoke English. They stressed that we would achieve success if we never forgot that material possessions can be lost or taken away, and that the one treasure you will never lose is your education. One summer, my parents decided to demonstrate this lesson in an unusual way. My mother took all five of us kids into the fields to pick onions for a few weeks. She wanted us to know what life in the United States was like for many Mexicans without an education. As children we loved the dirt, the burlap sacks, the onion smell, the bumpy truck rides and meeting other kids. However, I fully internalized her message and vowed to live a different kind of life— one of continuous education.

I graduated in the top three percent of my high school class in Greeley, Colorado. Greeley is a medium-sized farming town with a university, ranches and a meat-packing plant. My graduating high school class of 250 students included two African American students, a couple of dozen Latino kids and over 200 Caucasian peers. My school was far from diverse. I received thousands of dollars in college scholarships, including a four-year Air Force ROTC (Reserve Officer Training Corps) scholarship to attend the University of California at Berkeley. In four and a half years, I completed my degree in architecture. Along the way I held leadership roles in the AFROTC Cadet Corps and the Cal marching band, in which I played the trombone.

Upon graduating, I was commissioned as a military officer—a second lieutenant—in the U.S. Air Force. I served for over nine years, first as an aviation student, then as a navigator, then later as an instructor navigator. I flew onboard KC-135 refueling jets to all points of the Earth, which awakened my deep attachment to our planet. The soul-stirring environmentalism that comes from thousands of hours of flying and enjoying a bird's-eye-view of the globe is difficult to describe. From the jet, the earth's oceans and nations passed beneath me in a matter of hours. Going halfway around the globe took only sixteen hours. It is a small world we share. My consciousness rose gradually over nine years—an intense and life-changing time.

I have become a fervent recycler. I take public transit whenever possible. I teach my children how to grow vegetables at home. I teach my daughters how to turn lone socks into fashionable clothes for dolls to demonstrate creative reuse, just as my *Mami* (mother) taught me.

I am deeply curious. My professional life is filled with learning about different technical systems. First I learned and used radar, avionics, electrical, communications and navigation systems in the cockpit of military airplanes. Later, in my corporate global marketing career, I encountered legacy and IP-based communications systems, networking technologies, user interfaces and other related topics. I pride myself on consulting with experts to expand what I learn through my own reading and research. It's what I've always done.

For this book, I satisfied my curiosity by learning in some depth about the industries addressed in each interview. I wrote about the status quo because I wanted readers to understand each innovation in that context. How can you appreciate an innovation, or a groundbreaking development, without understanding the industry as it exists today? Ann Matranga, my good friend and developmental editor, wisely advised me to summarize (not explain) the industry information and lingo. Her advice helped me shorten each chapter significantly. Yet I've done the research to understand the industries you'll read about in this book. At the companion website, www.latinnovating.com, I offer you several unabridged chapters with more depth on these industries if you too are curious.

The success stories you're about to read do not often make it into the mainstream media. Such stories would force a change in the conversation about Latinos in America. Certainly it would be clear that many Latinos are successful business people, starting and growing companies, creating jobs—not stealing them, and adding significantly to the tax base—not taking money out of the system.

Sadly, many Latino youth in America never see leadership role models. Many parents encourage their kids to take jobs after high school instead of pursuing higher education. This is partly driven by the financial needs of the family. In greater part, it is because many families lack knowledge of the plethora of Latino role models who pursued higher education and succeeded. It is difficult to take the long view when you've never witnessed someone like you achieving success in the long term. When these stories escape the mainstream media, Latino youth are robbed of role models and the tired stereotypes persist.

I decided to help steer the conversation in a new direction.

This book provides inside stories from the Latino business community and its ties to the new green economy. You will meet people who are doing what immigrants have always done in this great nation—applied their hard work, talent, innovative thinking and creative spirit to improve America for *all* Americans. However, there is an additional element propelling these leaders forward—culturally-ingrained environmental advocacy. The book provides ten powerful role models for our youth—ten more reasons why the bet on education is one you can win.

You are about to meet a diverse group of Latinos whose families trace back to four different nations. I'll share where and how they grew up, and their first glimpses of environmental advocacy. You'll learn about their educational paths and decisions, and about the status quo in their industries. You'll read about their companies, organizations and inventions and the effect they are having on their communities and our nation. Each chapter ends with actionable resources and advice so you can begin to emulate these successful leadership examples.

These are some of the stories that follow:

Carmen Rad found a way to produce zero-waste promotional banners and billboards to reduce fumes and waste in landfills. She's leading the transformation of her industry.

Rodrigo Prudencio is a partner at a venture capital firm that has been singularly focused on funding new energy innovations since 1997. In our new greener economy that is dependent on constant innovation, he found the best place from which he could affect real change, after a professional journey rooted in environmental advocacy and action.

Rosamaria Caballero-Stafford launched a national eco-consulting company that has already trained over 700 independent eco-consultants around the nation. They determined that the best way to green our nation is to green one home, one business at a time.

Robert Zardeneta is leading a social justice organization that combines green building techniques with youth leadership training and college residency programs. He's saving lives while greening communities.

Frank Ramirez is contributing to massive energy reduction with methods that include a way to run air conditioning systems off the electrical grid during the hottest days of the year. He is helping to convert our antiquated electrical infrastructure into a sustainable "smart grid."

These are just five glimpses into the fantastic journeys taken by the innovators whose stories you'll read here.

Mitch Posada, my fellow NSHMBA member, wanted to draw attention to sustainable consumer practices for the Latino community.

Mitch told me that he's been asked why he cares about environmental and social responsibility issues. "Don't you people pretty much stay focused on immigration issues?" is a question he's been asked point blank. Is this what most of America believes about the Latino community? This book is going to change that conversation.

There are people in pockets across America who are in denial that a shift toward sustainability is necessary. Some people like things the way they are because the status quo has been good to them. I met one such woman in Virginia last summer at an oyster roast. She was an 82-year-old, conservative southerner who had owned several businesses. I mentioned I was writing "the first book at the intersection of the green economy and Latino entrepreneurship," which would be honored the following week at an event in Washington D.C. She responded, "This whole green economy thing is going to kill our country. That Obama—he's taking us down. Did you know that because of those newfangled light bulbs, a factory here in Virginia is closing and 250 people are going to lose their jobs?"

I asked her why she thought that factory should stay open. Why should it continue to manufacture products that consume more energy than necessary? Would it even make good business sense to keep cranking out old inefficient bulbs when consumers are choosing to buy more efficient products? She had no answers.

This brings me to an important point: this book is written primarily for high school and college students seeking information and examples to make wise choices about future career paths as our American economy undergoes massive transformation. Professionals who find themselves in mid-career transition will also benefit. Anyone who enjoys human interest stories filled with amazement, serendipity, inspiration and accomplishment will also enjoy this book. It is my intention to encourage environmental entrepreneurship among those entering the workforce now and in the next several years. Showcasing stories of those who once worked for corporate entities but left to improve upon the status quo just might motivate others to do the same.

There is an ongoing guitar theme through the book, represented by a guitar icon in each chapter. Here is why I chose to use this symbol. In one of the stories a father says to his son, "*Es otra cosa con guitarra.*" Loosely translated, this means "It's another thing with a guitar in hand." The essence of the story is that a guitar is what makes music possible. The guitar is also an important cultural icon in the Latino community. You can talk or you can act—those are your choices. You can talk about music or you can pick up a guitar and actually *make* music.

The people in this book hold the metaphorical guitar—they made a bet on *education*. Education has proven to be the instrument of power enabling them to act. With that in hand, they are equipped to play the music, to take the action, to stop talking about sustainability and actually create it. You'll see their educational achievements highlighted with a guitar icon to remind you of this important analogy.

This country is beginning to redefine its economic future. Let's show off the success stories of the Latino immigrants who arrived in the United States decades ago. Let's meet their children who are now achieving their own American dreams, applying their talents to create a sustainable, green economy for us all. Let's examine who is behind many of the innovative solutions that are changing traditionally wasteful practices in a variety of industries. Let's learn about the individuals who are creating green American jobs for all Americans. Let's see who is *latinnovating*.

Carmen Rad
Eliminating the Waste in Industrial Printing

*W*hen you can clearly connect the dots between formative childhood experiences and adult entrepreneurial pursuits, it is pure poetry. Carmen Rad's story is one such tale. Carmen was born on the island of Puerto Rico. She remembers seeing litter around the island and trash washing up on a beach. Her awareness of living on a finite piece of land triggered a question in her young mind. She remembers asking herself, "Where does all this trash go?"

Carmen recalls childhood discussions with her optimistic mother, Ana Maria. "She would always tell me, 'Carmen, you don't need to be the secretary—you can be the president. It's all within your reach.'"

Carmen calls her mother a constant source of encouragement, who is highly creative and an excellent, living example of reuse in action.

"One year at Christmas time, she gathered all these branches," Carmen describes. "She made a display stand. She sprayed her little tree and hung ornaments. She combined random objects into a beautiful piece."

Not from a wealthy family, Carmen says, "When you're not as privileged, you find a way to reuse. Not doing so affects your family's bottom line. Plus, it was important for us to think about where things went after we used them. It was important to try to reuse them. I learned it from being in a small space as a little girl."

"My mom is the one who taught me to reuse everything," she states.

"Was that because we were poor or was it because we were 'green'?" This question reveals a common theme among the interviewees in this book—about conservation practices in their childhood homes.

Carmen says that even today, her mother always finds someone else who can reuse things she is finished using.

"She will give away even a single T-shirt to avoid throwing it away," she says.

Ana Maria moved to the United States so her two daughters could be educated here and have more opportunities. When Carmen was two years old, they moved to New York City. Carmen remembers that Coney Island was very dirty, with trash and pollution on the beaches around the city. She recalls the unsafe conditions and littered beaches during outings with her family, wondering if this was the trash from Puerto Rico washing up in New York.

"I worried about getting cut, because I liked to walk barefoot," she remembers.

When Carmen was five years old, her mother remarried, to a construction worker in New York. Six years later, the business and construction boom in California brought the family west to Los Angeles.

Carmen's Educational Discovery
After graduating high school with a 3.5 GPA, Carmen enrolled at Cerritos College with aspirations to become a court stenographer. She quickly learned that such a career was not the best match for her.

"My teacher told me I did not have the personality for that job," she reveals. "When I was dealing with a murder case, I'd make all kinds of facial expressions, listening and reacting to the gory details of the case. I was not as reserved as the other girls."

Outside the classroom, she found she was even more different than her peers.

"I was so much more expressive. When watching water polo games, the other girls would be lined up, sitting and watching. I'd be hanging on the fence yelling 'I love you!' at the players."

Fortunately, her teacher spoke up and offered to guide her. She asked Carmen what else she liked to do. Carmen expressed an interest in fashion and design. The teacher suggested she take a fashion test.

"That is when I learned I was creative," Carmen tells. "Because of my high GPA in high school, I qualified for a government grant. I was able to get into and attend an elite school, the Fashion Institute of Design and Merchandising (FIDM) in Los Angeles."

While studying at FIDM, Carmen frequently spent time in the job placement office.

Carmen says, "The person in charge of that office was a Latina. I was in there every week looking for a job. I did modeling. I was exposed to so much information. I got to work in a high-end showroom and in a children's showroom. I also saw the low end of the fashion industry. I had a chance to travel. By the time I graduated, I had a huge portfolio. Plus, the work helped me pay for school."

Carmen graduated with her degree in fashion marketing and design and headed out into the fashion industry.

Life After College, Early Business Lessons
Shortly after graduation, Carmen learned that Calvin Klein® was looking for a representative in its L.A. showroom—someone bilingual with showroom experience.

Carmen explains, "People from Mexico and South America were coming to shop in L.A. Calvin Klein needed to communicate with the clients from these markets. Plus, I fit the jeans. I was a clean-cut, attractive Latina, and I had the showroom experience they needed." She landed an exciting job as a showroom representative for Calvin Klein.

"It was 1986. The only Latinos on the entire floor were me and the cleaning lady," Carmen recalls. "I started to see I was in a cutthroat industry. I started to see what it would take to move up."

"I knew I would be limited where I was," Carmen reveals. "I was a Latina working for someone else. I had seen so many different collections. I read their last names. None sounded like mine."

Carmen decided to move on. She got a job as an independent representative for a multi-line showroom with assorted collections from different designers. Various buyers came in to see the branded lines. One of the buyers who frequented that showroom, Masoud Rad, would eventually become Carmen's husband.

To learn the next part of Carmen's story, which would eventually lead to her decision to start her own business, I joined the couple in their new downtown L.A. location. It's a brick-exterior structure built in 1903 and located in the city's Enterprise Zone. Just blocks from the Fashion Institute where Carmen went to college, it is surrounded by other creative businesses in different industries.

We visited on the second floor in a fantastic, bright, open space. A glossy, dark wood floor adorned the vast space that made up a 24,000-square-foot facility. An eye-catching motorcycle decorated in one of Carmen's latest designs was a few feet away. It provided the only clue to the huge printing operation below us on the first floor.

Carmen and Masoud shared that they met again at the California Market (called California MART by insiders) on 9th and Olympic. This is the place that bills itself as "the hub of L.A.'s style industries." By that time, Masoud was a fashion designer with his own collection of clothing that sold at Macys®, Nordstrom®, I. Magnin® and other high-end retail stores. He designed beautiful men's shirts that hung next to very upscale clothing lines. Masoud had grown up and gone to university in the United Kingdom. He says, "Fashion in L.A. was a little bit behind in comparison to Europe."

With his printing and textiles background, plus his overseas connections, he had seen the need to make men's fabrics more exciting. He printed unique material and created beautiful, short-sleeved shirts for men. "We did really well with that for awhile," he says.

They were engaged two months after they met and married six months later.

"We went through a light recession in the '90s and then the stock market crashed," he recounts. "I had clients affected in Mexico and South America. Suddenly the business was no longer profitable. Plus, we were too young to know how to manage it properly."

He shut down that first business and went to work for AT&T®. Americans were discovering and buying cell phones. Carmen continued to work for independent showrooms until one day something sparked her brewing entrepreneurial spirit.

Thinking on her Feet

The story of how Carmen started her own company, first called CR&A Apparel, is quite instructive to anyone interested in owning his or her own business. There are "wannabe" business owners who research and analyze details forever before taking any action. Some get so paralyzed by the fear of potential failure that they never actually start a business. Then there are people like Carmen, who think on their feet. They see a need, see the open door and quickly step through.

Here's what happened. While working for an independent showroom that specialized in creating promotional clothing, Carmen got additional insight into the cutthroat nature of her industry.

"We were importing 11,000 shirts to be embroidered by someone else," she shares. "I had a friend at the client site. She called me to congratulate me on the deal going through. I told her I did not know about the deal, because my boss hadn't mentioned it to me. He hadn't told me that we'd won their business. Strangely, I couldn't find any paperwork about the transaction. Without it, I wouldn't get paid. I began to sense a pending ethics problem. I later learned that my boss didn't want me to know about the deal—he wanted to deny me my commission."

Carmen continues, "One day, my friend's boss (the client) shared that he had just learned (from Carmen's boss) that the merchandise he needed would not make it to the states in time for the client's event. Apparently, it was stuck on a boat in the middle of the ocean."

Wanting to solve her customer's problem, Carmen tapped into her professional network.

"I told my friend's boss that I could get the same exact items from someone else in time for the event. I knew who had what merchandise."

Carmen didn't have the cash on hand to make the quick transaction happen.

"So I asked him to give me a cashier's check for $285,000," she recounts. "I needed it to buy the merchandise and have it delivered on time."

Because he knew Carmen well and knew she could solve his problem, he gave her the check.

Carmen explains, "I did not have a business—yet! But I registered my business the very next day and that is how CR&A Apparel was created in 1993."

Carmen's quick thinking led to the birth of a new business. She is intuitive, decisive and willing to take the necessary action to make things happen.

Carmen continues, "My profit was $64,000 on this deal. By comparison, my commission with the guy who didn't want to pay me would've been $6,000. I decided that day I was never going to work for anyone else again. From now on, if I were successful or if I went broke, it would be because of me and my decisions."

She acknowledges, "That first step, to go out on your own, is very intimidating. But I had a lifetime of my mother's backing and her confidence in me. I also had my husband's backing."

CR&A Apparel began with two employees out of her home. The business involved purchasing ready-made goods and applying logos to the items. In the beginning, CR&A Apparel produced custom embroidery work and printed promotional items. When she landed an order from JCPenney®, she needed help and turned to Masoud.

"I asked Masoud to help me because he had an intense background in textiles and manufacturing," Carmen explains. "Clients were requesting items that were not commercially available. They needed custom-made clothing to promote their movies and events. He designed all of our custom-made items."

This is how Carmen and her husband came to run a business manufacturing promotional clothing together. Carmen handled the creativity, sales, marketing and production for promotional clients. Masoud handled the logistics. It's an effective division of labor formula that is still in place today—eighteen years later.

- AA, Fashion Institute of Design and Merchandising
- Graduate of the Management Development for Entrepreneurs (MDE) executive training program, UCLA Anderson School of Business

Staying Nimble and Proactive
A void in the market at the time was printing on polyester—a process called dye sublimation printing.

"We started doing custom prints for big names like Puma® and Ralph Lauren®," Masoud explains. "This included colorful jerseys for bikers. The only people doing it at the time were people with lots of printing experience, but no garment experience."

They started looking into printing on bigger formats, but the process was complicated. By now, Masoud and Carmen had seen much of America's textile manufacturing get outsourced to China. They saw the next trend coming. They watched as dye sublimation printing, typically done on articles of clothing made outside the United States, started shifting overseas too.

"We had to choose between joining those moving to overseas manufacturing or going into a new business," shares Masoud.

Raising two young boys at the time, the couple elected the latter. Large-format printing looked attractive and they decided to enter this industry. They felt that this sector would not be affected by China's presence in the international marketplace.

"We realized that this type of industrial printing had an altogether different dynamic. We found it's not impacted by China for two reasons," Carmen comments. "First, clients typically need custom-printed material quickly for their events. They need design and printing services to happen efficiently and fast. Second, they usually wait until the last minute to order. They can't miss their deadlines, yet they tend to give themselves very little time to get the work done. There isn't time to have the work done in China and shipped back to the United States." This buyer behavior keeps Carmen and what is now CR&A Custom firmly in the driver's seat to satisfy their clients' industrial printing needs.

The Primer on Industrial Printing

Dye sublimation printing is a process in which heat is used to transfer dye onto a plastic card, paper or fabric. The dye transitions between the solid state and the gas state without ever going through a liquid state.

Because it's a gas, a lot of the dye dissipates. The dye used in this process cannot be reused once it's on a panel, so the process is inherently wasteful. As a matter of fact, most of the dye may be wasted rather than used when printing. "The traditional commercial printing process from printing to disposal leaves a ton of waste," Carmen describes.

"Sublimation is when you print to paper first, then transfer to fabric with heat," explains Carmen. "There's a backing to the sheet and the backing is also waste. A heat transfer process then prints the graphics and lettering on the vinyl or polyester material which forms a permanent bond. You can never wash it out."

To appreciate the transformation that Carmen is leading, it helps to understand the current printing and disposal processes. For example, consider the huge banners you see outside car dealerships and exhibit halls. Those banners are typically ordered, printed and used for just one event. They are usually made of PVC vinyl, and though they can technically be recycled, the process to melt the PVC is detrimental to the environment. Plus, the recycling process involves taking apart the mixture of several materials within the banner. It's simply not cost effective. Because they cannot easily be recycled, they end up in the trash.

The industrial printing industry also creates items designed to catch your attention from a distance like billboards, car wraps, window graphics, wall graphics and trade show displays. These are also typically one-time-use items with a short commercial life and then forever in the landfill. Plus, the inks most commonly used to print on those items contain solvents. They have an unpleasant odor and add bad elements to the air we breathe.

Carmen and Masoud explain that there are three types of industrial printing processes in use today: lithographic offset printing, screen printing and digital printing. Every product can be printed using any of these techniques. The digital technique is quickly overtaking the other two processes. Smart investors put their money not in lithographic or screen printing, but in digital printing. That's exactly what the Rads did.

Masoud states, "At a trade show in 2003, we saw a giant version of a digital printer we currently had, with which we printed samples. My first thought was to bring that in to do sublimation. We played with it for a year and got familiar with the technology. We did about $30-40K that year in digital printing of larger formats, but it wasn't enough to pay for the machine in the first year. However, because the machine was a major capital expense, other businesses our size couldn't afford to get a machine like this. So we started selling to our own industry while still doing dye sublimation of clothing and textiles. Others would get orders and we would do the printing for them."

Note the "first-mover" advantage. The first to adopt a new technology when it's available is in a position to capture new revenue from clients desiring the new approach. It's a marketing differentiation for them to be able to offer what others cannot. In addition, the first mover is also positioned to offer services to competitors who want to offer these new services, yet have not made the capital investments in the new equipment. The Rads' experience makes for an excellent example of this advantage.

The forces of globalization have truly impacted this small business. In 2005, the World Trade Organization directed the U.S. government to end the subsidies that American clothing manufacturers had been receiving to stay competitive against Chinese manufacturers.

"Overnight we lost a twenty percent advantage we'd enjoyed over Chinese competitors," said the Rads. Soon thereafter, they shipped their last clothes printed with dye sublimation.

"Then we started focusing on marketing our new products using our new equipment," Carmen shares. "We had relationships in place and we just kept servicing those clients with new products."

Toward Less Wasteful Practices

"We've really been innovating in this area. We had been thinking about greening the printing process long before the equipment was invented to make it possible," says Carmen.

A heavy hurricane season hit the United States in 2005. Watching news coverage of the hurricane in the Caribbean and seeing all the tarp tents on television made Masoud and Carmen wonder, "Could we print on a truly recyclable knitted medium like a tarp?"

Tarps are made of polyethylene, the most widely used plastic. Polyethylene is in our plastic shopping bags. It's easy to recycle, unlike PVC vinyl. And some categories of polyethylene are biodegradable when exposed to UV (ultraviolet) rays from sunlight.

"We had polyethylene tarps created in white, but they did not lay flat. We had different samples of the material made, brought them back and ran them through the machine. The solvent-based inks did not stick to the new material. So we had a material that could finally be recycled easily, but we could not print on it."

Remember that today most banner printing media are made of a combination of nylon thread and PVC. You cannot separate the two materials in order to recycle them.

From the beginning, Carmen and Masoud have been intent on exercising thought leadership in their industry, while reducing waste as well. They had to go through the creative thinking, experimenting, failing and trying again, all along the way. Finally, they got the UV inks to stick to the new material.

"We wanted to create a material of only one compound, one plastic," says Carmen. "For a trade show, we made a mock-up to show that industrial printing could be done on this eco-friendly material. It went over very well."

"Then we learned that Hewlett-Packard® was developing a printer for eco-friendly UV inks. These inks are better for the environment because they don't emit nasty fumes into the air," Carmen shares.

The HP commercial printer, called the HP Scitex TJ8500, is engineered to prevent fumes from escaping into the atmosphere during the printing process. Carmen volunteered CR&A Custom, Inc. to be a beta site for HP's new invention. She became one of the first industrial printers in the United States to buy the machine from

Hewlett-Packard. "We made an investment of $750K in 2006 to get the machine delivered here. We also shared the new material formula with a few manufacturers that were able to produce it."

This combination of media, equipment and ink has revolutionized CR&A's large-format printing processes, becoming entirely green. The material the company first tried out five years ago is now common in large format printing. Innovation indeed comes from smaller companies. However, there were still some remaining obstacles.

"Our original idea was to use this new, fully-recyclable material to print billboards and other large items," Carmen tells. "Two billboard manufacturers are now using it, so that is good. But the problem is that nobody is recycling this material afterwards."

Why is this? The act of recycling billboards is not yet built into the habit pattern of people who take them down. Apparently, billboard companies have chosen this new material because it is cheaper to install—not because it's eco-friendly and fully recyclable. CR&A produces billboards in one continuous piece. Instead of paying two or three people to do a multi-piece installation, they can pay only one person. This behavior frustrates environmentally-minded innovators like Carmen. She's disappointed with companies that make choices based only on cost and do not consider the environmental impact of the cheapest choice. What's most frustrating to small business owners like Carmen and Masoud is the hypocrisy surrounding the green movement: that companies and agencies talk green, yet unlike CR&A Custom, they don't live the values.

The Rads told me about a government agency requesting bids for a printing job. The project initially required that the print job be done with eco-friendly materials. The agency ultimately selected a non-eco-friendly printer once that printer told the government buyer that a greener approach would be too expensive.

Carmen asks, "What message does this behavior send to us small business owners who are investing capital to make our industry more eco-friendly with new innovations?"

What if eco-friendly printing became the expected norm instead of the exception it is today? One possible step would be for *all* corporations and government agencies to specify in their Request for Proposals that materials *must* be biodegradable and printed with UV inks and the like. That's truly the greenest possible industrial printing combination.

"We need people to step up and do the right thing so we can reach critical mass," says Carmen. "We are making investments in new machines, and need more incentives to make these investments. As an example, we have purchased a machine that can print with latex (water-based) inks. A great way for government to get involved would be to provide low interest loans to help printers acquire new, eco-friendly technology. There are fifty-year-old printing machines still in use out there."

Carmen adds that there are truly green companies making real investments in their green credentials through focused actions. Carmen touts the green credentials of customer Coors Light®, to which she sold a program last year. Coors Light bought the original 300 rolls of new material CR&A created. The idea was that Coors would distribute these new banners to their clients for their usage in their promotions. When they were finished with the banners, they would send the banners via UPS to a recycling plant for conversion into pellets. While I was visiting Carmen and touring the printing floor, the Coors Light banners were rolling off the huge printers.

"Coors Light has really stepped up and made more eco-friendly printing choices," Carmen states. "They've made a financial commitment and continue to work with us as part of their investment in their green initiatives."

However, Coors clients who received the eco-friendly banners didn't go to the trouble of sending the banners in for recycling. Human behavior apparently is the biggest obstacle. There are other realities to balance too. The Rads shared that there is a research and development-focused company that now puts an enzyme into a material called BIOflex®. The PVC in the BIOflex product at the landfill is biodegraded by this enzyme in about nine months. Yes, it's currently more expensive to buy this new material, and traditional solvent-based ink machines can't print on it. Printing on BIOflex requires using UV-inks, which are also pricier. Therefore, Carmen and Masoud offer this eco-friendly BIOflex printing option to customers who want it and need it for their green credentials.

Carmen points out, "Biodegradable printing materials are more expensive than recyclable ones, but they truly leave no waste. This difference is very important to me and to the customers who buy our products."

CR&A also offers its customers traditional, less expensive printing processes. The company maintains a healthy and realistic balance to reduce waste and move its customers toward more sustainable choices, while continuing to serve the unique needs of its long-time customers. The Rads realize that not everyone is ready to take the green leap.

What motivates Carmen to focus on innovating and moving forward with eco-friendly printing? "It's important. I know what I'm producing," she answers. "Now that the technology is evolving and solutions are being created, I feel like I'm doing my part. Now it is time for people to step up, put their money where their 'green' mouths are and move their business to eco-friendly industrial printers like us."

The Company Today and Going Forward

The business Carmen started in a moment of sheer ingenuity has grown to a full-service, large-format, digital print production and visual display company with thirty employees in a fabulous, recently renovated facility. It has a large, dedicated space for the creative design team on the first floor near the small army of huge machines cranking out large-format pieces. The company is certified as both a minority and woman-owned business. It prints trade show and exhibit booth graphics, plus graphics for vehicles, windows, walls and floors. It specializes in the digital printing of large items like billboards, indoor/outdoor banners and signage for sports stadiums.

When I visited Carmen, she was just finishing a big job for Major League Baseball® and was taking her son to a game that night. I envisioned her enjoying the baseball game while also admiring the work she and her team produced for the stadium. Carmen proudly shares that her company still serves some of its original clients from 1993, such as Disney®, Coors and Nike®, along with newer brands like Xbox®. She showed me a photograph of a recent project, a huge job that transformed the entire Disney monorail train into a bright yellow submarine to launch the park's Finding Nemo® ride. [Photos I took of Carmen's creations are at www.latinnovating.com.]

The key message on the CR&A website is crystal clear: "CR&A produces green printing: organic, recyclable and biodegradable."

Carmen touts several characteristics of their differentiated approach to industrial printing. "We utilize a water-based coating technology, which contains no volatile organic compounds and is completely earth-friendly. CR&A's products are especially environmentally sound—they're made of 100 percent organic materials and are naturally recyclable and biodegradable. The manufacturing processes of our green substrates comply with all ecological certification, exceeding 2020 compliance."

Not many industrial printers today exceed compliance standards a full decade in advance. Carmen is doing it today for the largest visual displays they produce. "We are the first to market a full range of earth-friendly printable media up to five meters wide, recyclable polyester textiles and biodegradable organic textiles up to 196 inches wide."

Carmen's business has received numerous awards for its continuous innovation and commitment to greening industrial printing prac-tices. In 2007 the U.S. Department of Commerce named CR&A Custom the *Manufacturer of the Year*. In the same year, the California Hispanic Chamber of Commerce named her business *Latina Business of the Year*.

Other awards include:

- *Green Firm of the Year* honors from the City of Los Angeles Minority Business Development Council

- *Supplier of the Year* honors from the Southern California Minority Business Development Council

- The *Rising Star* Award from the National Association of Women Business Owners

The last award on the list recognizes "a woman entrepreneur who has established a critical milestone in her business and has displayed high potential for enduring entrepreneurial success." Recently, the Congressional Hispanic Caucus Institute (CHCI) recognized CR&A as a leader in our green economy at the Latino Innovation Recognition session in Washington D.C.

Today, Carmen's business works with major corporations in the United States, Puerto Rico and Dubai. She's aggressively pursuing future business deals with organizations that make a "high frequency of purchases" of large banners. Ford®, Honda® and Toyota® have yearly marathon sales events and need new banners printed every few months. These are the types of businesses she wants to attract. Carmen wants CR&A to be the most successful industrial printer satisfying the needs of corporations with superior printed products, while leaving zero residual waste when the event is over. The little girl from Puerto Rico who once wondered where all the waste goes has grown up and is doing her part to produce less of it.

Your Path into a Green Industrial Printing Career

When they transitioned from the apparel business to the printing business, Masoud retrained their employees instead of replacing them. It was the right thing to do and created a tremendous sense of loyalty from their staff. Instead of having only their initial sewing skills, their employees have new, upgraded technical skills. When I asked Carmen and Masoud what advice they have for those interested in this dynamic industry at the beginning of its green transformation, here's the advice they shared:

For high school students interested in the commercial printing industry:

- Study graphic design and commercial art.

- Get a minor in business.

- Have a great resume and learn how to present yourself well. First impressions matter.

Carmen says they only hired in-house graphic designers with bachelor degrees. In addition, she says, "Business school helps if you are an entrepreneur. It also helps if you go work for someone else, because you understand the owner's pain. You become a better employee."

To position yourself for this highly technical industry, Carmen says, "Become an expert in Adobe Illustrator®, PhotoShop® and InDesign®. These are the tools of the trade. Read *Big Picture* Magazine. Join the American Printers Association and the Printing Industry Association. Subscribe to their blogs and newsletters."

For college students, take the same advice as above, plus, "While in school or right afterward, get an internship at a major company even if the pay is low. Consider the temporary low pay as an investment toward valuable, hands-on experience. Then, if you do not move up, take the experience and the network you have established to a mid-size company that can use and build on your skill set. Work for an ad agency. Get a letter of recommendation whenever you leave a job."

For the college graduates that Carmen interviews, work experience is important. She wants to see both what you can do and *who you know*. Mention your professional and personal networks during your job interviews!

"Their networks matter to me. Does the candidate have relation-ships with vendors or clients who interest me? Who are their friends and colleagues?"

For those in mid-career transition, she says, "Take college classes to become an expert in the current tools of the trade. You can't break into this without at least knowing how to use those design tools. This industry is technical, but the classes are easy to find. Read *Big Picture* Magazine and *Digital Output* too. Join the associations mentioned above. You've got to be able to 'talk the talk.'"

An existing network that you can tap as you enter this industry is a tremendous asset for those in mid-career transition. Networks built up over a decade or more will interest employers like Carmen. You've probably worked in different places and know many people who could be potential clients for a new employer. Tout your network when you make your transition.

If you are interested in owning your own business, Carmen suggests, "If you are a woman, join the National Association of Women Business Owners (NAWBO) and begin to network with the members in your local chapter. Join the Latina Business Association. Always have, and nurture, multiple networks."

Finally, Carmen reminds all readers, "Mentors come in different stages of life, different shapes and sizes. Learn from each of them but do not attach yourself to just one mentor. That is why it is important to join organizations and keep growing by meeting new people. Keep asking questions."

Carmen Recommends

- Check out www.cracustom.com to see what products can be printed using eco-friendly printing materials and processes.

- Read *American Printer*. Its mission is to be the most reliable and authoritative source of information on integrating tomorrow's technology with today's management. www.americanprinter.com

- Join the Printing Industries of America; read what they publish on their website: www.printing.org

- Read *Big Picture* Magazine, "the business of wide format." www.bigpicture.net

- Read *Digital Output*. www.digitaloutput.net

- Take a look at www.fidm.edu to learn about the creative college Carmen attended in L.A.

- If you are a woman, join the National Association of Women Business Owners. www.nawbo.org

- If you are a Latina or want to associate with Latinas in business, join the National Latina Business Women Association. www.nlbwa.org

- Note: The most successful business people are actively involved with multiple networks. Group with your gender, group with your ethnicity and of course network with people within your own industry. Always nurture diverse networks.

Company-owned photo by Leroy Hamilton

Carmen with her industrial printers and large-format eco-friendly banners
www.cracustom.com

Rodrigo Prudencio
Funding Innovations to Reduce Energy Consumption

*A*s a child, Rodrigo Prudencio traveled often through Latin America's developing countries with his family. His Bolivian-born parents insisted he speak Spanish while growing up in Chicago as the elder Prudencio completed his medical residency.

Reflecting on his early travels through Latin America, Rodrigo says, "When you speak the language and travel in those regions, you really get to meet the people. You are invited into their homes and get a different perspective from that of a typical tourist."

He pondered the differences in lifestyles of the people he met there versus his own in the United States. As he got older, he thought about the issues of poverty, economic development and environmental impact as Latin American nations continued to develop.

Rodrigo discussed policy questions with his father, who quoted from the book *Martín Fierro*, by 19th century Argentine writer José Hernández. He told Rodrigo that talk is cheap and action matters more. You can talk about making music or you can pick up the guitar and do it. "*Es otra cosa con guitarra*," became an important *dicho* (saying) in Rodrigo's life.

"I asked myself this question: 'How can the economic development of Latin America and the standards of living for its people both progress without damaging the environment?' I eventually came to see that if real change were to happen, it would happen through business."

Curves on the Path of Advocacy

These early experiences brought environmental advocacy to the heart of everything Rodrigo has done professionally. After graduating from Middlebury College in Vermont with a bachelor's degree in international relations, he became the director of the international trade program at the National Wildlife Federation (NWF). He led NWF's environmental advocacy efforts to reform the rules of international trade. It eventually became apparent that the type of change Rodrigo wanted to make in the world was not going to happen from within this non-profit organization. He moved to Washington D.C. to work for the U.S. Department of State. "In D.C., all my work was environmental. The inspiration was my travel through Latin America with my family."

Rodrigo's work at the State Department focused on a variety of global environmental negotiations. These included preparations for the Kyoto round of the Climate Change Convention during the George W. Bush administration. When the United States failed to sign the Climate Change treaty, Rodrigo began to wonder if working in a policy capacity would lead to the kind of environmental changes he wanted to see. He realized that to drive meaningful change, he needed to become a businessman. The *dicho* from his father resurfaced, *Es otra cosa con guitarra*. Rodrigo saw that he wasn't yet holding the metaphorical guitar—the power.

Rodrigo decided to attend the Haas School of Business at the University of California at Berkeley. He served as president of his class and concentrated on energy markets while earning his MBA. His graduate studies included research at Lawrence Berkeley National Laboratory.

- MBA, Haas School of Business, University of California at Berkeley
- BA in international relations, Middlebury College, Vermont

Guitar in Hand

Rodrigo shares, "After getting my MBA, my intention was to work at a company in the alternative energy space. I worked at a clean tech startup and helped them raise money doing business development work. The firm was one of the portfolio companies of Nth Power LLC. That is how I got introduced to this firm."

Nth Power LLC is a San Francisco-based venture capital firm that has exclusively focused on funding energy technology. "We've been backing and investing in 'green' startups since 1997, way before it was called 'clean tech.' Our founders believed that a convergence was coming: the deregulation of energy markets, severe resource constraints and new innovations in technology. They rightly predicted these elements were going to intersect," says Rodrigo.

The Primer on the Venture Capital Process

A venture capital (VC) firm is a group of people who invest money into newly-formed or already established businesses they believe will be successful. They want to put in some money (capital) early in the company's life, hoping that the eventual success of the company (the venture) will result in excellent monetary returns for their investors. Some VCs invest their own money as part of this process. Many are investing other people's money. Some of the best venture capitalists are those who have worked within businesses started by entrepreneurs. They have experienced the reality of creating something, looking for capital, acquiring it, managing it, hiring people, identifying markets, creating, marketing and selling products, laying off people and repeating these processes as capital ebbs and flows.

What does a VC do? The firm hears business pitches from entrepreneurs with ideas. They listen to an initial presentation by the company's leaders. Those leaders must answer the many questions that VCs must ask before considering investing money in a new, unproven idea. Examples of these questions are:

• Who is the executive team?

• What is the innovation?

• What do the financials look like from years one to five?

- How much startup capital is needed?

- Who will buy this new product or service being created?

- How much will they pay for this new product or idea?

- How will you market your product or service to your intended audience?

- Who will sell your products and services?

- What is the profit margin we can expect for these sales?

- How long will it take the company to become profitable?

Typically, only teams of entrepreneurs with well-thought-out business plans get opportunities to pitch in front of VCs. A VC can provide the startup capital to initiate a company's operations. That investment capital comes from a pool of investors who trust this firm to make wise investments with their money. You can bet that VC partners investing some of their own money will take great care in where they invest it, because they've got serious "skin" in the game. When a company receives this initial cash infusion, it can begin to hire its first employees.

Once a company is established and needs to expand, its management team may present its business case to a VC firm in hopes of securing additional investment dollars. When a VC feels a company has a credible plan, a promising management team, a solid strategy, an important innovation and an adequate and addressable market, the VC says yes and a deal is done.

If instead, the firm's partners have doubts or feel that key facets of the business plan are weak, the partners may say no. Or, if the firm believes the idea has potential, but the presented plan isn't adequate enough to deserve immediate funding, the partners can suggest improvements to the plan and ask the team to return in the future. A company that needs capital to continue operations and is not successful in securing new funds may find itself in the unpleasant situation of laying off employees. I've seen this scenario a few times in the last decade. I've been married to it. My husband has worked for various startup technology companies. Together, we've lived those happy "we-got-funded" days and the depressing "we-didn't-get-funded" days.

Indeed, the role of VC firms in funding new ideas is powerful and unparalleled. Some firms, such as Rodrigo's, only invest in specific sectors or technologies. They have a particular area of focus so that they capitalize on the business experience of the partners, the professional networks to which they have access, and their knowledge of trends in a particular sector. In clean tech, typically referring to innovation in the energy industry, VCs may choose to invest in several broad sectors: biofuels, energy efficiency, smart grid and solar.

Other firms have specific criteria that a business plan must meet to be funded, such as "double-bottom line" or "triple-bottom line" criteria. These require not only healthy, realistic profit projections, but also job-creation results and social responsibility (including environmental) components. The key knowledge an entrepreneur must have when seeking out VC firms for the pitch is an understanding of the area(s) of focus important to the VC. That way, the entrepreneur only targets firms interested in hearing those ideas. For example, an entrepreneur with an idea for a new type of athletic shoe sole should waste no time pitching to firms that only fund business software solutions.

The Best Venture Capitalists—Tips from the Inside

Because the role of the VC is so crucial to our new economy and because most high school and college students have never heard of this career path, here are some tips on the best paths to take to become a VC partner from two very active VCs. This is actionable advice from Latinos who want you to follow them into this career field someday.

Our first prominent venture capitalist, who is also a successful entrepreneur, is Eduardo Rallo. Eduardo is a graduate of Harvard Business School, owner of Farmácia Remedios, as well as several other businesses in the San Francisco Bay Area. Eduardo spoke on a panel I moderated at the Inaugural Silicon Valley Latino Leadership Summit that took place in the VC heartland near Stanford University. When I asked Eduardo to describe the ideal career path to VC partnership, here is how he answered:

"I did not know what a venture capitalist was until my senior year in college. But when I did learn about it, I felt I should be a businessman first. It's critical to get an understanding of what it means to be an entrepreneur or to be able to work in industry. You need to understand how difficult it is to build a company, how difficult it is to hire one, two, three people, and to understand the basics of what makes a business work or not work. Some failures are not bad. Many of the entrepreneurs I have backed in the past have had some successes and some failures. 'Arrows in your back' are sometimes pretty positive things, because these are things you would not do again.

Once you have worked in a company or had a chance to start one, that is a better time for you to decide if you want to take the path toward becoming a venture capitalist. You will be a better VC if you've had operational experience during your career. If you have done it yourself, it is easier to see eye-to-eye with the entrepreneur. You can add more value because you have a better understanding of what the business needs. In my experience, the most successful venture capitalists are those who understand they are part of the company and part of the solution to any challenges that may come up. They don't focus on criticizing the entrepreneur's errors. Instead they say, 'These are the opportunities. I can help you with this. I can connect you with that person.' That goes back to not only having the direct experience but also to exposing yourself to meeting people. This gives you a strong connection base that provides access to deal flow, to capital and a number of other valuable skills that will add value to the company in which you are investing.

I would never recommend that you graduate from college and immediately attempt to become a venture capitalist. Long term, that's not the best thing, even if you could get such an unlikely break. I recommend first becoming an entrepreneur or working for a corporation. Understand how difficult it really is to do that. Then, find your path toward the VC world."

Miriam Rivera also has valuable advice if the VC career path interests you. She is a former Vice President/Deputy General Counsel at Google® Inc. She now heads her own firm, Ulu Ventures. Because the VC world isn't exactly brimming with Latinas, it is important to hear the perspective of one who is in the thick of it. While speaking on the same panel with Eduardo, she shared the advice below. Here she details how you can follow her into this somewhat insular world. She paints a clear picture of what it takes, and of the successes and failures along the way that will ultimately prepare you to succeed as a venture capitalist.

> "The typical profile of a VC is a white male who went to Harvard or Stanford Business School. Using that reality, most of us in this room today do not qualify. If you are aiming to get into venture capital, it does not hurt to go to Harvard or Stanford Business School, because that's where most VCs come from.
>
> After I left Google and was planning my next career move, I realized 'Hey, I actually graduated from Stanford Business School.' I knew that step would help me establish credibility and gain access to a network of people experienced in venture capital. A VC's network adds great value to a company. You must have the same or higher quality network as anyone else in the business. This was not my master plan. I hadn't considered venture capital as a career path when deciding which school to attend. Serendipitously, it became an avenue available to me, having attended both business school and law school at Stanford.
>
> Another important thing I did that helped me transition into a VC role was to work at every stage of a startup company, either as a lawyer or as a business person. As an associate in a Silicon Valley high technology law firm, I helped to form companies, handling the legal aspects of their initial financings. Then I

worked in a major strategic management consulting firm where I learned how senior executives look at strategic business issues and worked on projects designed to improve their companies' financial performance. For example, we would help a company figure out how its market was changing, how to enter new markets, or how to create new product offerings that would generate more revenue from existing customers.

Finally I went into 'Startupville.' My first company dissolved after five years during the 'Bust' years in Silicon Valley (2000-2001). I cofounded a business with my husband, an engineer with a PhD from Stanford. The VCs didn't want a husband and wife working together, even if my skills would help grow the business. I left our startup in 1999. At times, it has been harder for me to be a woman, in contrast to a minority, in business.

Next, I joined a post-public company as an attorney before the peak of the high tech bubble in 2000 and went through the Bust there. The company more than quadrupled its staff size in my first year there. The next year they cut more than half the employees. I helped to save that company's financial performance by helping them offload a tremendous amount of real estate liability through the largest sublease done in California that year. This restructured the company's balance sheet so it could be profitable again. Simultaneously they reduced their legal team from 36 to 9 people. I was networking in case I didn't survive round four of the layoffs. That is when Google hired me, so it worked out well. Ironically, I was recommended for the position at Google by a friend I had to lay off at our startup company. I helped to grow revenue at Google from $85 million to $10 billion in five years, grew the legal team from 2 to 160 people worldwide, and grew the company from 160 employees to 10,000. I had grown with Google from pre-public to post-public to S&P 500 and Fortune 500 success story.

It has been a roundabout path to the VC world, but these experiences exposed me to every stage of a startup company's life, from formation to becoming a public company (or to dissolution). This background has been tremendously valuable in my new role. The entrepreneurs I work with now are excited to work with someone with a background in operating a company, rather than investment banking experience. They are thrilled that I can help them work through questions like 'This new hire isn't working. How do I turn this around? Should I find a place for him within the organization or do I have to get rid of him?' Or, 'We lost this customer or this round of financing. How do I make the tough decisions about how we are going to survive?'

One more thing: because you can never have too much preparation and education, I have joined the Kaufmann Fellows Program, one of the best VC training programs anywhere. Today, I am doing angel investing—I am investing my own money. This training will take me to the next level. I have found both the Kaufmann curriculum, and the relationship-building opportunities they offer, very helpful to my work at Ulu Ventures."

Rodrigo's Role in the Green Economy

Rodrigo is now a partner with Nth Power, involved in all aspects of the firm's operations including investments, investor relations and portfolio management. He led Nth Power's investments in Hara Software, Synapsense, Topanga Technologies and Terrapass. "Everything I do here at Nth Power is focused on finding companies that will lower the amount of energy we use," he says.

As you can see, this firm is highly focused on funding innovation to improve efficiency. This is consistent with Rodrigo's personal values. His passion for doing right by the planet extends deeply into his personal life. He calls himself an "obsessive recycler." He uses reusable drinking vessels, avoids waste and does all the little things that fortunately have become commonplace in some parts of our society.

"I've never needed a car for my commute, so I have a low carbon footprint that way. I do transport my family in a car, but not every day. I buy organics and locally raised beef and food." Rodrigo goes one step further by using carbon offsets for things he cannot avoid. "I buy them from a company we invest in called Terrapass." [Carbon offsets are certificates that represent projects that reduce carbon dioxide emissions; these projects counterbalance personal/corporate emissions.]

Rodrigo doesn't believe everyone should go straight to buying carbon offsets. Conservation matters much more. Instead he says, "The most important thing you can do is to do all the little things that collectively make a big difference every day."

This includes cutting (or eliminating) commute trips and walking more. It includes consuming fewer plastic shopping bags and switching to reusable tote bags. Turning out the lights and computers when not in use are big energy-saving steps we can do at home.

He continues, "Buying carbon offsets should come at the end after you've done all those things. There are real CO_2 emissions being taken out of the atmosphere with these offsets because standards are finally in place."

Rodrigo's greatest motivation to pursue this line of work goes back to his early experiences traveling in developing countries. "I realized very early on that if they followed the same economic development path as the United States, it would severely tax our planet. Now, as a father, I think of a different legacy."

Rodrigo believes that the message of *consume less* doesn't meet the aspirational psychology of the average human. He says that a message to *consume better* could work. It's about being aware of our choices.

"I'm concerned about choices people have in their appliances, their vehicles, their homes and businesses. When the government sets higher standards of efficiency, then people can consume what they want, while ultimately consuming less energy." Rodrigo's perspective is shaped by where he lives and works—in California, the state with arguably the most aggressive energy efficiency standards in the country.

He observes, "Energy consumption has been standards-driven in California. It's a great example of how consumption can continue to occur and how growth can happen, without energy usage going off the chart."

Rodrigo takes a firm stand on what he believes is possible, saying, "I refuse to believe that there's a trade-off between a better standard of living and our ability to use resources wisely. My job with my team here at Nth Power is to find the entrepreneurs who will make this possible."

It's comforting to know that people like Rodrigo and the investors at Nth Power are out there, laser-focused on finding (and funding) those entrepreneurs who will help maintain our standard of living while finding new ways to consume less energy.

When I asked Rodrigo about the innovation activity level he's seeing, he answered positively, "There are three to four times more entrepreneurs at work now in energy-related improvements than when I started. It's very encouraging."

Indeed it is. In my research for this book, I found that the amount of venture capital invested in alternative energy resources has increased steadily quarter by quarter. The Cleantech Group is an excellent source of information about venture capital investments in different clean technologies. This is a great way to watch trends and follow the money.

Rodrigo and Nth Power are making those decisions and investments, powering the innovation with capital that creates jobs. They are helping all of us maintain our lifestyles into the future while consuming less. Rodrigo finally has the *guitarra* in his hands and won't be letting it go any time soon.

Rodrigo Recommends

- Visit www.nthpower.com to learn about the portfolio of companies Nth Power LLC is funding today and how to submit a business plan.

- Visit www.terrapass.com to learn about carbon offsets.

For high school students interested in working for a clean tech company someday, Rodrigo recommends:

• Get involved in a local environmental or green space project. Lead a park cleanup. Start a recycling campaign. Work at an urban garden. Get close to big issues by understanding them at a local level.

• Get the big picture. The best and fastest lesson is to watch the movie *An Inconvenient Truth*.

• Learn the basics about how our energy system works and how it touches your life every day. [Note: You'll find specific resources to do this at the end of the chapter about Frank Ramirez and Ice Energy.]

For students currently in college and thinking about working for a clean tech company soon, Rodrigo recommends:

• Jump in! Find a company you like that is involved in something that stirs your passion. Find a role where you can make an impact.

• Start reading publications like *Scientific American* that will ground you in mainstream energy topics.

For professionals in mid-career transition looking to find an entry point in a technology sector of clean tech, Rodrigo recommends:

• Familiarize yourself with the different sectors that comprise clean tech. Read online publications that serve up great content on clean tech topics such as *Earth2Tech* (www.gigaom.com/cleantech) and *Greentech Media* (www.greentechmedia.com)

• Use your networks to find positions that link well to your job history and experience; clean tech jobs are like many other tech jobs.

For those wondering how one becomes a venture capital partner, Rodrigo recommends you:

• Work with a company and learn the ups and downs of a startup environment.

- Use your personal networks to meet a few venture capitalists. Learn what they do, how they got to where they are, and what advice they have for an interested newcomer.

- Keep your expectations at a realistic level; venture capital hiring is idiosyncratic and irregular.

Let's recap the advice from these venture capitalists: get a lot of business experience in a variety of settings before you pursue the very serious role of deciding which new potential business ideas get funded and which do not. This is sage advice from Rodrigo, Eduardo and Miriam to consider as the new American green economy expands. The opportunities for experience will truly be unlimited in the coming decades. If your heart is set on eventually becoming a VC partner after reading what Rodrigo does at Nth Power, take your cues from the other entrepreneurs in this book first. Then later make your way into the VC world, when you've built up a vast network and extensive operational business experience.

Additional Recommendations

National Venture Capital Association (NVCA)—this is a trade association that represents the nation's VC firms. Their site lists events, industry news, public policy highlights and information for entrepreneurs. It includes a featured section called "Venture-Backed Start-ups Are Hiring!" where VC-backed startup companies list thousands of open jobs across the nation. The listings include "clean tech" jobs among the startups. www.nvca.org

Cleantech Group LLC—this is a global research group that puts out frequent press releases about their findings, including how much venture capital money is flowing into which clean tech industries. Formed in 2002, they bill themselves as "the first-ever venture capital forum on clean technologies." www.cleantech.com/about/pressreleases

Look into the Kauffman Fellows Program whose stated mission is to "identify, develop and network emerging global leaders in venture capital." The program is a two-year, full-time apprenticeship that includes mentorship and practical leadership experience. It is based in Palo Alto, California and administered by the Center for Venture Education. The Center describes itself as "a 501(c)(3) post-graduate educational institution dedicated to fostering entrepreneurship throughout society." Read about founder Ewing Marion Kauffman, and his legacy of promoting "economically independent individuals who are engaged and contributing citizens." Appreciate the $6 billion in venture capital investments the Fellows have made so far, plus the hundreds of new enterprises, the $15 billion in annually recurring revenues and the creation of 50,000 jobs. www.kauffmanfellows.org/overview.aspx.

Rodrigo in the San Francisco office of Nth Power LLC
www.nthpower.com

Rosamaria Caballero-Stafford
Your Local Green Friend

*W*ho starts companies that grow into highly profitable global enterprises? Who asks crazy questions like, "Why not train women to sell plastic storage containers to their friends in their own living rooms?" That odd question turned into the first Tupperware® Home Party in 1948. More than sixty years later, Tupperware is a multibillion dollar enterprise of 817,000 independent sales representatives serving over 100 markets.

Can you take that model of selling, apply it to benefit the environment and create many small businesses around the country? What kind of big thinker would have that idea and pursue it? Could it be the daughter of Cuban immigrants who arrived in this country with nothing but their education?

The Young Girl
Eduardo Caballero and his wife Raquel were attorneys in Cuba who ran their own law practice. As an educated couple with no children, they were at the peak of Cuban society—life was good. In October 1961, everything suddenly changed. They were forced to flee Castro's Cuba and eventually arrived in Dallas, Texas. The following year they moved to New York City with no material possessions and limited English skills. Three years later, their daughter Rosamaria was born. By the time Rosamaria was eight years old her parents had started their own business. They owned a national radio rep company, helping acquire national advertising dollars for Spanish-language radio stations that had previously never received a penny of it. A big thinker, Eduardo was the first person to convince Proctor & Gamble® (and other major consumer companies) to buy ad time at

radio stations reaching Spanish-speaking Americans. The Hispanic media industry considers Eduardo a pioneer.

Little Rosamaria worked side-by-side with her mother and father, learning the entrepreneurial ropes from a very young age. She learned that commissioned sales people can make a nice living and that owning a business was a great thing. As she worked with her parents, the family's entrepreneurial heritage was passed on to Rosamaria. Her maternal grandparents were from Lithuania and Poland. They had immigrated to Cuba and had owned retail businesses there. She grew up knowing her parents and her grandparents were entrepreneurs. Even in so-called retirement, her father started yet another business, MasMusica TeVe, which was like a Spanish-language MTV. Rosamaria worked with her father in that business too.

Rosamaria looks back now and recalls they lived quite a green life in New York City. They lived vertically, not horizontally. They used mass transit and walked a lot. As the child of uprooted Cuban refugees with nothing, Rosamaria always heard the message that education was the most important thing in their lives.

"I was told, 'whatever you have in your head cannot be taken away,'" she relays. Her parents had already proven that with an education, a person who loses everything can pick up and start over again. "I always knew every material thing we had could be gone tomorrow," she reveals.

As she got older and her parents' business thrived, life became comfortable. Rosamaria was fortunate to live a middle class life and attend private school in New York City. "My mother would rather pay for the best education possible than put food on table," she shared. "It was that important."

The Educational Journey

Rosamaria attended an all-girls middle school. Her high school graduating class had just 32 students. Her Cuban-educated parents could provide no insight or guidance into navigating the American university application process, nor could they suggest what to study in the United States. Rosamaria knew one thing that she wanted—to attend a small college for her undergraduate studies rather than a huge university. She was accepted at Wellesley College outside Boston. Wellesley bills itself as "the world's preeminent college for women" and "one of the most selective liberal arts colleges in the country." This is the college that educated Madeline Albright, the first woman ever appointed to serve as the U.S. Secretary of State. Hillary Clinton, the Secretary of State in the Obama administration, is also a Wellesley graduate.

It's a beautiful thing to see the daughter of Cuban refugees ultimately end up in such a distinctive educational setting. Rosamaria chose to study political science and economics in preparation for becoming a lawyer. Her mother had wanted to become a lawyer in the United States. Sadly, that dream didn't come true for her.

"Since my early high school days, I knew I wanted to be an attorney," Rosamaria stated. "I knew the training in law school would help me no matter what I decided to do."

As a Wellesley woman, Rosamaria had high expectations of herself. She dreamed and imagined big. Look no further than her college application essay as proof of this. "I had to write a headline and subsequent story about a news event that had just taken place," Rosamaria recalls. "I wrote that I had been selected as the first female head of the United Nations." What possessed her to write such a thing? Clearly she was strongly influenced by three high school summers spent abroad in Switzerland and London. Her eyes had been opened wide during her travels; she imagined working in Europe. She had also gained exposure to Europeans' attitudes toward the environment. She was acutely aware of how greatly that mindset differed from that in the United States.

When Rosamaria graduated, she immediately applied to law school. "I thought I would do something internationally, because I speak Spanish, French and some Italian," she said. But her plan changed. She met a young man named PJ during her first year of law school. Two weeks after passing her bar exam, and two weeks before he started his graduate degree, they married. The new Wellesley-educated attorney practiced in Boston while her husband pursued his MBA at Harvard Business School.

- BA, Political Science and Economics; Wellesley College
- JD, Georgetown University Law Center

Because PJ wanted to work in manufacturing, the couple moved to Michigan. Rosamaria worked in-house for Masco, based in the city of Taylor. The head of international sales there was coincidentally a Cuban. She did contract work for his department and helped set up Delta Faucet in Mexico. By the ripe old age of 26, Rosamaria was an attorney with international corporate contracting experience. The pieces were falling into place; soon her entrepreneurial spirit would demand to express itself.

The Direct Selling Model in the United States

Rosamaria and PJ started a direct sales company called Green Irene®. The company trains independent representatives to provide eco-consulting services and products directly to consumers. The sale typically takes place between the eco-consultant and the customer.

Before delving into specifics about the company, it is important to understand the long tradition of direct selling in the United States. The Direct Selling Association (DSA) is a prominent trade group representing the interests of 200 of America's direct selling companies, their representatives and consumers who buy from them. DSA ensures that member companies' marketing and sales practices are conducted with the highest level of business ethics and customer service. After months of scrutiny, Green Irene earned its DSA membership.

Some companies, like Avon® and Tupperware, have a commission-based compensation structure; some others have a recruiting-based compensation structure and some have a combination of the two. In the former, sales reps keep a percentage (their commission) for each service or product they sell. In the recruiting-based model, sales reps make money recruiting more people to sell for the company. Green Irene is commissioned-based.

According to DSA, 73 percent of all annual direct selling is done in private homes. Perhaps your parents have purchased or sold products in your home? Rosamaria is riding this wave with her company.

Americans become independent sales representatives for direct sales companies to supplement an existing salary, to earn a full-time income or to buy products at a discount. Others do it to meet people or to gain recognition for sales achievements. The numbers are staggering. According to DSA, in 2009 there were 16.1 million direct sales representatives in the United States who collectively sold $28.33 billion in goods and services in the worst economy in seventy years. That's an average of $1,762 per sales rep. Many reps make enough income to make direct selling their full-time jobs. Many others get involved on a part-time basis—simply to make extra money. Collectively, these part-time activities add up to one giant economic engine in this country.

Given this phenomenon Rosamaria and PJ have brilliantly taken a proven business model constructed for perpetual growth and longevity, and applied it to the green economy. Now, every neighborhood that has a "Tupperware Lady" or an "Avon Lady" can also have a Green Irene helping to green the community's homes and businesses.

The Eco-Consulting Industry
The eco-consulting industry is in its infancy. Many people are calling themselves green consultants and helping others "go green." There is no national certification program, nor is one currently required. It is the early 21st century equivalent of the 1849 gold rush that brought so many people to northern California. Green is the new gold, and the numbers support this. In mid-2009, the *New York Times* ran an article titled "Make Me Greener, Please." It cited Colorado-based GenGreen, which offers a national directory of businesses marketing themselves as green. GenGreen stated that it had over 3,000 listings using the term "environmental consultant" —up from 657 consultants when GenGreen started the database in 2007.

This is nearly a 400 percent increase over a two-year period. Will that growth rate continue?

To learn more about the eco-consulting trend, I met with Carolina Miranda, founder of Cultivating Capital LLC, a San Francisco Bay Area business consulting firm specializing in helping women business owners develop sustainable businesses. The firm's services include marketing, business planning and sustainable business practices. Carolina recently graduated with an MBA in sustainable enterprise from Dominican University in San Rafael, California. This was the nation's first Green MBA program focused on sustainable business practices.

Carolina told me the Bureau of Labor Statistics has predicted the growth rate in management, scientific and technical consulting jobs in the ten-year period ending in 2018 to be 83 percent [Source: *Career Guide to Industries*, 2010-11 Edition]. The field is so new, however, that there's virtually no research predicting growth rates for eco-consulting.

She says business owners and managers are hiring eco-consultants because, "Sustainability is very new in the business world. Executives are realizing they don't have that expertise. For example, how do you green your supply chain? How exactly do you become more energy efficient? How do you convey your initiatives in your marketing? These are new skills that are needed in the business world. There is a large demand for people developing these skills now—they can advise businesses on, and lead the necessary changes toward, sustainability. If a business wants to implement sustainability initiatives, it makes sense for them to hire a consultant who has experience in that area."

"There are a lot of people trying different things," Rosamaria says. "There are many ideas floating around. Eventually, there will be a shake out; a consolidation." She points out that while diverse ideas are good, it is in *how* a model is executed that matters most in the long run. Different opportunities will present themselves and emerge. "We are learning today what people really need to green homes and small businesses," she explains. "We are learning what they will actually pay for when they want to do something positive for the environment. This early collective knowledge will certainly lead to more innovation."

In the *New York Times* article, clients who have hired eco-consultants were quoted as follows:

• "I liked the idea of someone coming in and analyzing our lifestyle and taking a look 'under the covers'."

• "It was customized to my way of living and I could ask questions."

You might like the idea of running your own business that could create similarly satisfied customers. Rosamaria has developed the training and infrastructure to help you do this in your own community.

The phrase "think globally, act locally" has always been part of my adult consciousness. I first saw those words on a bumper sticker when I was in college in Berkeley. For me, the phrase "think globally" means that individually we *must* think about the big picture when we think of our planet. We must imagine it as the precious and finite piece of real estate that it is. When you think globally, you think the opposite of selfishly. You think and act as if you are a citizen of an interconnected global community—because that's who you truly are.

I clearly remember thinking about those words "think globally" when flying as a crewmember in the cockpit of the military refueling jet I traveled in for over seven years. For one deployment, we flew for 16 continuous hours, direct from Spokane, Washington to Riyadh, Saudi Arabia. In that time, we felt as if we were hanging in the sky, watching our beautiful and mostly-blue globe spin below us. We called those missions "skyhooking," as in hooked onto the sky. We would say, "We're skyhooking it to the desert tomorrow." We would watch cities, then states, then countries, then oceans, then icepacks and then continents pass by our cockpit windows, seven miles below us. Our family members perceived that we were going very far away, to the other side of the world. From the aviator's perspective however, we had a deepening sense that our Earth is very, very small. Crisscrossing the globe extensively gave me the sense of awe at how small a place humanity shares. Think globally.

"Act locally" helps you avoid becoming overwhelmed by feeling responsible for protecting the entire planet once you appreciate it as a whole. It means instead of trying to act globally, take action where you live, where you feel comfortable doing it and where you're likely to keep doing it. Then, if everyone acts locally, we are collectively acting globally. It's simplistic, but powerful. Within this framework of thinking globally and acting locally, you can understand and appreciate Rosamaria's contribution to our green economy.

Rosamaria's Unique Idea: Your Neighborhood Green Irene

"What made us start our business was very much related to Al Gore," Rosamaria states. "His book and movie, *An Inconvenient Truth*, really enlightened us. We decided we needed to do things differently."

Al Gore's book, *An Inconvenient Truth: The Planetary Emergency Of Global Warming And What We Can Do About It*, (Rodale Books, 2006), opened the eyes of the world to the factual, scientific data about global warming and its long-term consequences. In 2007, Rosamaria and PJ sold the television business they ran with her father Eduardo. That spring, they read Al Gore's book.

A few months later, their family rented an apartment in Argentina for a month. "I remember the hallway lights were off when coming out of the elevator," Rosamaria recalls. "There was a motion sensor that controlled the lights there; lights were only on while someone was in the hallway. Here in New York, hallway lights appear to be on all the time. I remembered that in Europe all restaurant bathrooms had sensor-based lights too. I was suddenly very aware of the different attitudes toward energy consumption and environmental responsibility in the United States compared to other countries."

Later that year, Rosamaria and PJ traveled to my part of the country, northern California. They saw the Altamont Pass with its thousands of wind mills harnessing the wind blowing in from the Pacific Ocean. They got exposed to the trend toward solar tubing, and other elements of the green economy. Rosamaria and PJ thought about what Al Gore's movie meant and what it might do to the American public.

"We felt the movement was not going to mainstream," she said. "It had the potential of staying within the granola crowd. There was just too much information, too many changes needed, and it seemed too extreme for many people."

"PJ is a big picture guy. Like my father, he has the ability to see the opportunity for an entire industry to develop. As an example, we started a web development company back in 1994, when people did not yet know what the Internet was."

Rosamaria and PJ had digested Al Gore's book and the subsequent movie. They reflected on the differences in attitudes about the environment between Europeans, Latin Americans and North Americans. They began to get clarity on how they might respond. Their idea began to crystallize into a way that they could act locally and also teach many others to act locally. Plus, they wanted to address the sense that there was too much information, that the problem was too big and nobody knew where to start to make a difference to the planet. Indeed after watching Al Gore's documentary, many people feel completely overwhelmed and are unable to take any specific action.

"We felt that people would need someone to come into their homes and offices and be practical," she reveals. "We felt that to take action, people would want someone to come in and tell them exactly what they really needed to do to make a difference. Homeowners would want someone to lead the way and hold their hand."

In addition, Rosamaria says, "We felt the product part was missing. For example, replacing your CFL bulbs isn't necessarily simple. When you start looking at all the different types of light bulbs in your home, you start to realize that some CFLs work in chandeliers, some with dimmer switches, and some don't work in either of these. There are lots of choices. Expecting homeowners to take the time to figure out this minutia would surely result in most not making the bulb switch due to a high level of perceived difficulty in doing so."

The other possibility is that the homeowner experiences "analysis paralysis." After researching all possible options he is frozen into inaction and never replaces his light bulbs. Rosamaria and PJ decided to start with educating homeowners and providing the path to fully greening their lifestyles. They could provide baby steps for those who needed to just get started. They could offer a full makeover for those ready to fully change their consumption patterns.

"We started with doing Green Home Makeovers," she explains. "This involves your trained local green friend, your 'Green Irene,' coming into your home to review your current lifestyle. He or she takes a look at your household energy consumption, your water consumption, your household cleaners and your transportation usage. The eco-consultant then makes specific suggestions in a written family plan to reduce your overall carbon footprint." This is all about acting locally.

The consulting component is a key part of Rosamaria and PJ's business. People pay $99 for a Green Irene consultant to come into their homes and review how they use products and resources. If the report recommends products, the homeowner may choose to purchase or not. Eco-consultants do not have a monthly sales quota; they receive a substantial portion of what they charge for their consulting services, and they receive a commission on product sales. It's an innovative approach to greening the world one home or office at a time—with a local touch. "We started this business because we felt the greening process needed to be a local, grassroots effort," Rosamaria explains. "It was not going to get much traction as an initiative based in a corporate office somewhere far away from everybody."

Rosamaria describes her Green Irene LLC business model this way: "We build businesses. We provide the infrastructure, the training and a website for each consultant. We do the order processing, the research, the support and the fulfillment. We maintain the inventory. We ship the products. We help individuals create a local eco-consulting business in their community. We help people power their practice. Think of it as a 'business in a box.'"

There are three types of people who become Green Irene consultants:

1. The Classic Stay-at-Home Mom. The Tupperware lady meets the green economy. This is the mother who has a few hours to be a business person during the day while her children are at school. She may be at home more than the average woman working outside the home. She is already adopting green practices for her family and wants a toxic-free living space. "We thought it would give them the opportunity to have their own flexible business, something they'd be proud of doing," Rosamaria reflects. "These people are local green friends already. We give them the education and training they need; they spread it throughout their neighborhoods, communities and their circles of influence."

This was the demographic the company originally sought to reach, the most likely place to find its first eco-consultants. They quickly learned the market was much broader, with 28 percent of Green Irene consultants being men.

2. The Wannabe-Green Professional Working in a Non-Green Career. These are the people who have regular, full-time jobs doing work that is not related to environmental initiatives. Yet, they are passionate about greening their communities. They are part-time Green Irenes on weekends, and some evenings. Some want to make a full-time career out of this activity someday.

For those of you in high school and college who have a fully-loaded class schedule, you could emulate what these people do and use your weekends and some evenings to have a part-time business. You could work as much or as little as you like, building up a clientele and gaining some expertise.

3. The Multi-Faceted Greening Consultants. These consultants already have a business and a client base, or they are looking to start a business. For them, the Green Irene Home or Business Makeover is another valuable offering in their sales toolkit. This is one more consulting service and product set they can offer their clients. These are energy auditors, professional organizers, real estate brokers with a green designation, LEED-accredited professionals, green cleaning companies and baby-proofing specialists. Many of them are already advising homeowners in some capacity. Directing the conversation toward ideas about how to green their lifestyle is relatively simple.

Green Irene completely trains new eco-consultants—no educational prerequisites are necessary. The initial training alone is thirty hours long. Rosamaria says a common element among their consultants is a passion to green their communities. "They have to believe in what they're doing," she states. "They must practice what they preach. That's what attracts people to us. They have to *get it*."

If they do, and if they have excellent green lifestyle credentials themselves, they will likely be much more successful than if they do not. Rosamaria believes that taking small, doable steps over time is a much better approach than trying to take huge steps all at once. The latter can lead to being overwhelmed and lead to failure.

Operating on a commission basis shows Green Irene's commitment to actually improving the air and the environment within a home. You get paid for teaching homeowners and small business owners how to be green and consume less. Convincing your friends to become a consultant like you is *not* part of the equation.

Why the brand name Green Irene? "We wanted the word green in the name. We started with searching available domain names even before we tackled the trademark search. It was silly—Green Irene—it rhymed. As we thought it over, the name stuck and we realized it would help give us a local voice," says Rosamaria. "It also made it personal—your friend Irene has a familiar sound to it. It was a deliberate business decision to help differentiate the company's approach to eco-consulting."

"We're the only eco-consulting firm—and the largest—with a national presence," Rosamaria states. "That is because we have a national brand and a consistent message. Green Irene is friendly. She's your local green friend. There are companies who train eco-consultants to go out on their own but they have no cohesive identity. We're cohesive and consistent." Rosamaria and PJ have created consistent, easily accessible, reasonably-priced training, supported by a robust corporate infrastructure. They're happy to have their Green Irene training set the standard. Their eco-consultants can say they are certified and trained by Green Irene, which has a growing reputation across the nation.

A few months after the home makeovers kicked off, Green Irene eco-consultants began asking if they could do green makeovers at business locations. Thus, the Green Business Makeover was born. "Our target is the small and medium-sized office," she explains. "Our tagline is 'your outsourced chief sustainability officer.' This means we know that smaller businesses need what large corporations have when it comes to sustainability initiatives, including someone to plan and execute them. We also know they won't be able to afford a full-time staff person to do these things, so they hire us."

The innovation continues. Rosamaria believes that providing consulting services for small businesses has some exciting potential. For a business consulting with Green Irene, the benefits include reducing operating costs, creating a healthier workplace for employees, and attracting green-minded customers and business partners.

In the spring of 2010, Green Irene LLC announced a joint venture with the Green Business Bureau (GBB), headquartered in Houston, Texas. Marcos Cordero is CEO and co-founder of GBB, which describes itself this way:

> "GBB is a national third-party program providing certification for businesses that follow environmentally responsible practices. Started by a group of environmental and business professionals who recognized a need in the marketplace for a trusted green certification for small-to medium-sized businesses, GBB fosters environmental awareness among businesses and promotes business practices that are both environmentally responsible and commercially beneficial."

GBB and Green Irene stated in their joint press release that they are "creating the industry standard for a reasonably-priced green business certification for small-and medium-sized businesses…Together, we now offer a comprehensive, in-person, audited green business certification."

These two organizations teamed up to recognize and publicly reward small businesses taking concrete steps toward becoming more efficient in their consumption of natural resources and in adopting sustainable business practices. Truly green businesses want to separate themselves from the "greenwashers"—those who market themselves as green yet are not. This certification helps them differentiate. In teaming up with GBB, Green Irene is now able to offer business makeovers specifically tailored to over twenty different industries. The certification process begins with an in-person consultation with a Green Irene-trained eco-consultant and ends with GBB issuing the certification. After that, Green Irene-trained eco-consultants return at a predetermined frequency. They ensure continued compliance with certification requirements. It's a perfect synergy for business owners who want to boost their green credentials and gain recognition for their efforts to 'go green.'

This joint venture has led to further innovation at Green Irene. Through these talks with GBB, Green Irene has been able to revamp the original Green Business Makeover to make it very specific for different industries. The list of specific industries in which they are working together includes:

- Automotive repair
- IT and engineering
- Dry cleaning
- Hotels and motels
- Nurseries and greenhouses
- Photographers
- Professional services
- Hair care and salons
- Cleaning services
- Construction
- Food services
- Landscape services
- Office supplies
- Printers
- Retailing, wholesaling, trading
- Event planning

- Dental and medical practices
- Gyms and health facilities
- Day care centers
- Cafeteria services

The business model is evolving in other ways too. "In addition to individuals, we have businesses enrolling as Green Irene eco-consultants," Rosamaria explains. "We have one company that already has three locations."

I spent some time looking at the extensive product line Green Irene carries. I couldn't help but wonder how long we'll have the green versus non-green tandem manufacturing of things like light bulbs, household cleaners and the like. How long will that approach make sense? Rosamaria believes, "Eventually, hopefully, there won't be a distinction between green and non-green products anymore. They will all be sustainable."

For now, there is a distinction, so this Latina and her husband continue to innovate. "We have just started manufacturing our own products here in the United States, a line of Green Irene enzyme cleaners. We have six products. We promote them as effective, safe and sustainable. First, they actually do work. Second, we put all our ingredients on the label so you know what's in there. Third, they are designed with a sustainable product cycle in mind. We didn't want to ship giant containers of liquid around the country, so we created a refillable packet system." Instead of shipping large containers of household cleaners, the company ships a small pouch of concentrate. This approach requires less energy to produce, less energy to package and less energy to transport. It leaves very little to dispose of at its destination. Green Irene truly executes the greenest possible business practices. Would she have it any other way?

Clearly Rosamaria, PJ and Green Irene are onto something very promising and very much in demand. Will they be the first Tupperware-like success story in the green economy?

My mother sold Princess House Crystal®, Tupperware and other products during my childhood. I once had my own misconceptions about the commissioned direct selling model. After learning the facts, the code of ethics and seeing industry statistics, I am instead impressed. I see the effectiveness of the model and respect the economic power these companies have. Remarkably, in 2009 the nation's 16.1 million direct sellers outperformed store-based retailers. They also showed a stronger year-over-year growth rate.

Green Irene has been approved by the Board of the Direct Selling Association as a full member. It is also a Platinum-level Green Business Bureau-certified business and a member of the Better Business Bureau. High standards in customer service and a commitment to ethical business practices are important to Rosamaria and to the sellers her company has trained. What is special about her model is that when the sales transaction is done, an entire family, or an entire employee group, has learned how to use energy more efficiently, how to conserve water and how to make choices that are better for the planet. Whether or not the customer purchased products in addition to the makeover, they purchased knowledge. They now want to be more responsible with natural resources. That in itself is a wonderful foundation on which to build a business in this new economy.

I asked why of all the things Rosamaria could be doing, she's doing this. "During that 2007 transition year, we thought a lot about what we wanted our next business to be about," she recalls. "We had two daughters, ages twelve and seventeen. We wanted our business to be something we could be proud of. We wanted to help people make the changes needed, and teach them how to do it, making the world a better place for our kids. We wanted to feel good about our industry. The side benefit was that we could continue to be entrepreneurs and help other people become entrepreneurs too. It's turning out to be something of which we are truly proud." People are beginning to notice. Green Irene was recognized by the Congressional Hispanic Caucus Institute last summer at the Latino Innovation Recognition session of their Public Policy Conference.

Rosamaria Recommends

For high school students, Rosamaria offers this advice: "Get involved at the community level. Get experience and learn about green issues in your community. Look at your school. Is it acting in a sustainable manner? Are they using bottled water? If you see something you don't like, get with your administration to make changes. Ask 'what products are the classrooms being cleaned with? What are we breathing in here every day?' What about the packaging in the cafeteria? Does your school have an environmental club? If not, start one!"

Rosamaria's teenage daughter is a great leadership example. She led a computer recycling program at her school. Together with the parents and an e-waste facility in the Bronx, they cleaned out the school's closets of old computer equipment, and families brought their e-waste from home as well. She later led a similar program at the neighborhood level.

"Host a shredding event. Get a shredding company to come to your site and have people bring their documents. There's so much you can do."

Is your family recycling? Are they turning lights off? Do you have a family action plan? Do you lower your thermostats? These are ways to raise your consciousness and improve your own environment that may lead you to wanting to do the same for others. Rosamaria also recommends that high school students read the following books:

• *Hoot* by Carl Hiassen

• *Ishmael* by Daniel Quinn

• *Worldchanging: A User's Guide to the 21st Century* by Alex Steffen

• *Dr. Art's Guide to Planet Earth: For Earthlings Ages 12 to 120* by Art Sussman PhD and Emiko Koike

Watch the following:

• *Planet Earth*

• *e²*: PBS series narrated by Brad Pitt. Each hour-long episode focuses on a specific subject like transportation, food, design and energy, among others.

Visit these sites online:
- www.epa.gov/students
- www.epa.gov/careers/stuopp.html#hs

For college students, Rosamaria makes these recommendations. Read:
- *Hot, Flat and Crowded* by Thomas Friedman
- *Cradle to Cradle: Rethinking the Way We Make Things* by William McDonough and Michael Braungart
- *Earth: Making a Life on a Tough New Planet* by Bill McKibben
- *Unbowed: One Woman's Story* by Wangari Maathai
- *The Omnivore's Dilemma* by Michael Pollan
- *The World Without Us* by Alan Weisman
- *Worldchanging: A User's Guide to the 21st Century* by Alex Steffen

Blogs/Magazines:
- *Mother Jones*—www.motherjones.com
- *OnEarth*—www.onearth.org
- *Inhabitat*—www.inhabitat.com
- *Grist*—www.grist.org

Watch:
- *Planet Earth*
- *The Cove*
- *An Inconvenient Truth*

Join:
- www.350.org
- Clinton Global Initiative University—www.cgiu.org/about

- WWOOF (World Wide Opportunities on Organic Farms) www.wwoof.org

- Any on-campus environmental organization

Green Irene has designed a program enabling college students to become consultants. "We have just launched a campus consultant training program. Now students at all college campuses can go through our training program. They can speak to homeowners in their college community and provide paid consulting services. They can help their neighbors go green with services and products. It is a great opportunity to get some hands-on, practical experience. It is your own flexible business and you'll have a great item on your resume."

See if the training is something you'd like to do to generate cash for yourself over the summer or part time during the school year. Visit www.greenirene.com.

For professionals in mid-career transition, Rosamaria makes the following recommendations:

"First, ask yourself this question: do you have a passion for greening your community? Realize that you are doing this for the greater good and there is a financial benefit for you too. But more than anything else, you need to believe in this and live it. If you don't already have the education for this sustainable business, we can provide that. We've created the program so that you don't need outside training. If you want to do it full time, look at our business consulting services training. The residential services are more part-time and part of that tool box as well. Create your own green business."

Read the books by Frieman, McDonough/Braungart, McKibben and Pollan recommended above, as well as:
- *The Necessary Revolution: Working Together to Create a Sustainable World* by Peter M. Senge, Bryan Smith, Nina Kruschwitz, Joe Laur, et al.

- *Green to Gold* by Dan Esty

Blogs/Magazines:

• *Green Inc.*—www.green.blogs.nytimes.com

• *Fast Company*—www.fastcompany.com/topics/ethonomics

• *OnEarth*—www.onearth.org

Join Net Impact. This is an "international non-profit organization with a mission to inspire, educate and equip individuals to use the power of business to create a more socially and environmentally sustainable world." www.netimpact.org

Other Resources:
To learn more about the direct selling model, visit the Myths and Facts section of the Direct Selling Association site. www.directselling411.com

Gen Green Life is a national directory of businesses marketing themselves as green. www.gengreenlife.com

Wellesley College offers an Interdepartmental Major in Environmental Studies. Located online at web.wellesley.edu

The nation's first Green MBA in Sustainable Enterprise is a program focused specifically on sustainable business practices. This program is taught at Dominican University in San Rafael, California (north of San Francisco, across the Golden Gate Bridge.) Find it online at www.greenmba.com.

Company-owned photo by Danielle Stingu

Rosamaria with her line of Green Irene enzyme cleaners
www.greenirene.com

Luis Rojas
Harnessing the Sun's Power to Benefit Schools

*L*uis Rojas exemplifies the characteristics of an entrepreneur who never let life's disappointments limit his potential. Instead, on more than one occasion, disappointment led him onto a more satisfying and profitable path than the one he had been walking.

Luis was born and raised in the Boyle Heights area of East Los Angeles. He lived in a house on Evergreen Avenue that had been in the family since 1932. He lived with his mother, Consuelo, and his two older sisters in this house that was owned by his Uncle John. The arrangement allowed the family to live inexpensively and the rent never went up. They lived a frugal life out of economic necessity. They turned the water off while lathering during a shower to save money. They made sure the lights were off to lower their utility bill. They reused everything in the household to the maximum extent possible.

"When you have only one of something, whatever it is, you take great care of it," he says. "Besides, you don't know you're poor until you leave the neighborhood."

Unfortunately, Luis' father, Roberto Rojas, was a part-time dad. After his parents' separation, Luis visited his father at his auto mechanic shop, spending many weekends there during the school year. During the summer, he worked alongside his father almost daily. The other influential man in Luis' life, his "Tio Johnny," had been a gang banger who planned to enlist in the military and fight in the Korean War. On the evening he was to leave for boot camp, he was in a horrific car accident and lost his arm. Instead of boot camp, he earned his GED, and then his college degree in accounting.

"Losing his arm saved his life," Luis sums up. "He worked for the Los Angeles Unified School District as an accountant. Later, he became an Enrolled Tax Preparer and started a tax preparation firm in the garage of his home. He became an example to all members of my family."

The entire family lived in the same neighborhood. Many cousins, aunts and uncles lived on the same block. The adults all gave the same advice to Luis as he became a young man.

"Uncle John was my *nino* (godfather)," Luis shares. "I remember growing up and being told to 'go be like your *nino*.'"

Luis attended Euclid Elementary School, Hollenbeck Junior High and Roosevelt High School—all public schools in East L.A. He was a quiet kid with many friends in high school. He didn't seek out leadership positions. As he started applying to colleges and universities, his father became ill. To help out in the family business, Luis decided against moving away to attend a large university. Instead, he enrolled at nearby California State University-Los Angeles. During his summers, he attended East L.A College to reach his educational goals faster.

Much later, Luis realized the importance of having his uncle as a strong, positive role model in the family, in a world mostly devoid of good role models for young Latino men. This uncle, a gang member turned accountant turned business owner, was the only family member with a college degree at that time. Naturally, Luis decided to major in accounting. He simply did not know about other areas of study, but he did know accounting had worked out well for his uncle.

The Accountant in College and Beyond

"I found my voice in college and became a campus leader," Luis says. "I was involved in the Hispanic Business Society and became President. We had fundraisers and dances. I ran for a college governance seat, and I won a position as Representative of the School of Business and Economics to the college's Associated Student Government."

His senior year internship was as an auditor with the U.S. Department of Health and Human Services. At a nationwide department event in San Francisco, a man asked Luis where he'd gone to high school. When Luis answered "East L.A." the man asked if he was a *cholo*, a gang banger. Luis became furious. His boss calmed him down and helped Luis to see the opportunity to educate others and lessen the stereotyping about East L.A. Luis realized he would be doing this his entire life. There are things presented in the media about the larger East L.A. community that can only be dispelled by meeting people like Luis (and Robert Zardeneta in a later chapter of this book).

Luis plugged away at his accounting classes. Nothing came easy. "I did not have a high GPA. I was not an 'A' student. I did not test well. But I learned something every day and ultimately graduated."

His parents came together to celebrate his graduation. Luis was the first in his immediate family to graduate from college and only the second after his *nino*. "We had a big festival in our backyard, with *mariachis*," he recalls. "To this day, I have a picture of me with my parents in my cap and gown."

When Luis graduated, he had eight job offers. "I had an outgoing personality," he states. "I got offers from banks, CPA firms and telecommunications companies. A recruiter named Joe from Capital EMI Records offered me a chance to become a record promoter. I played the trumpet and had been in band. I thought working in the music business would be great. He said that most promoters are guys with MBAs, but he thought I could do a great job. Unfortunately, months passed and I didn't hear back from Joe."

Later, at a banquet for graduating seniors, Luis found himself standing at a major fork in his road of life. A female recruiter from Capital EMI sought him out, apologized for her colleague Joe dropping the ball and offered him the music promoter job on the spot. She said he would live in Miami and have an expense account. She emphasized that he'd be part of the emerging 1980s Latin music scene with groups that included Gloria Estefan and the Miami Sound Machine. Luis turned her down because he had already accepted a position at First Interstate Bank (now part of Wells Fargo). The lady was incredulous that he would choose to be an accountant at a bank instead of working as a promoter at a major music industry label. She asked him to think it over: Miami, expense account, single guy, music business. Luis admits that fear of the unknown kept him from seizing the opportunity and moving to Florida. He had never been far from home. He rejected her offer and never looked back.

- BS, business administration (accounting), Cal State University, Los Angeles

Luis began his career at First Interstate Bank and continued his education through in-house corporate training programs and on-the-job training. He joined Toastmasters International®, an organization devoted to helping people become more comfortable in front of an audience. He did a lot of public speaking. He took many classes, including some in technology. After working for a few years, Luis began to explore obtaining his MBA. In 1991, he had completed a set of interviews and was on his way to pursuing his MBA in Chicago. Suddenly his father collapsed in the mechanic shop and died of a ruptured ulcer at the age of 73. Luis was only 25 years old.

"My father's death made me become an entrepreneur," Luis shares. "I realized that an MBA degree would prepare me to work for someone else or to maybe eventually start a business after working for someone else. I realized I already had a business. I moved the business to a different location and began to grow it."

By now he had become the highest ranking Latino in the real estate division of the bank, and had audit, finance and asset management experience. First Interstate had offered him a position in the San Francisco Bay Area but later retracted it for budgetary reasons.

"A vendor of the bank asked me to start a new business with him," Luis says. "I started an asset management company and named it

UREO Services, Inc. We took bank foreclosures and sold them for the banks. We made commissions once we sold the properties." Luis ran the operations, brought in the clients and hired and trained the staff (including his older sister Virginia Campos). When the firm became profitable, the senior partners decided they wanted Luis out, so they made his work life difficult. As part of his exit strategy, Luis fired his sister in order to prevent his partners from doing so, telling her he planned to create a family business. Luis' clients followed him into his new venture.

"My buddies from the American Association of Hispanic CPAs helped me start my next business. One helped me incorporate my company and another set up my books, all in exchange for pizza and beer." The takeaway from this is to surround yourself with friends whose professional skills complement your own. Your diverse network will be there when you need it. Associating only with people who know what you know does not accomplish this.

Luis and Virginia managed assets for eight different banks. As the banks consolidated, customer numbers declined. They began looking for a different path. Luis knew the construction companies they hired made good money. Therefore on weekends, Luis, his mother Consuelo, and his sister became the laborers rehabilitating homes from which families had been evicted. "Usually those homes were quite messed up," Luis recalls. "We gave them curbside appeal. The real estate agents would see me on weekends installing toilets, doing the hard labor needed. Then on Monday, they'd see me again as the asset manager."

Luis' entrepreneurial spirit was in full force now and he was just getting started. He met the Facilities Director of the Montebello School District, an older fellow Roosevelt High School graduate. Luis was contracted to do small jobs for the district. One day, the facilities director was frustrated with a spreadsheet and Luis volunteered to help him with it. Surprised that Luis wasn't "just" a contractor, the director then learned that Luis was also a banker, an auditor and an accountant. As a result of solving the director's spreadsheet problem and already having proven his firm's skills as a school contractor, Luis ended up managing $170 million of the district's money on various capital improvement projects. His business took off from there. Seeing an opportunity and jumping all over it is what successful entrepreneurs do.

What is Solar Energy?

Writing this book has allowed me to satisfy many curiosities. I have often wondered about different industries and technologies the news mentions, but rarely explains. I have wondered how electricity is transported to where it's needed. I have wondered exactly how solar panels work.

As I interviewed Luis, now a solar energy developer for school districts, I saw the need to understand how the sun's energy, which we experience as heat, becomes electricity. How does that energy get converted, powering so many things? Here is the short course on how solar panels work.

What is a solar panel and how does it collect the sun's energy? A solar panel is made up of many photovoltaic (PV) cells. Instead of ending up as heat as most sunlight does, some of the sunlight that reaches a solar panel is converted directly to electricity. This happens because the silicon materials in the cells are designed to capture elements of the sun's energy (photons) and cause them to create electricity. Because each cell can only convert a small amount of energy into electricity, many cells are needed to work together on a panel to convert a significant amount of rays into usable electricity. [If you're curious to know specifically what these photons do when they strike the material on a photovoltaic cell, visit this great site: www.eia.doe.gov/kids/energy.cfm?page=solar_home-basics]

On average, today's panels only convert 14 percent of the sunlight that hits the surface into electricity. That means that 86 percent of the sunlight is *not* captured and converted; it remains as heat or is reflected away. Certainly we can do better.

"The future is the light-weight, thin-film panel," says Luis. "It rolls out like a paper roll on the rooftop. But today, this thinner solution still has a very low efficiency rating. The engineering challenge is to improve the efficiency of the thin film. That's the problem our engineers need to solve." Thin-film solar cells, using a fine layer of semi-conducting material, have traditionally converted about twenty percent of the sunlight. They harvest electricity with much less physical material, which is a huge advantage. A small amount of thin-film material can absorb the same amount of sunlight as traditional silicon PV cells, and it's less resource-intensive to produce.

Luis predicts that the adoption of solar energy will grow fast. However, Luis reminds us, "This is not new technology. It is available in other countries already. Vendors from other countries are coming into the U.S. market with cheaper solar panels and undermining our manufacturers."

That's okay. We want our American advantage to be in innovation, not in competing for the manufacturing of commodities getting cheaper by the day. The race is then for the science of the medium used to convert the sun's energy into electricity. As scientists and engineers experiment with different materials, they achieve different levels of efficiency. Materials that yield higher conversion levels to electricity are extremely exotic and too expensive to mass produce. In one example I found, the efficiency of silicon cells was quadrupled from eight percent to thirty percent, but at *100 times* the cost because of the materials needed.

Here are some problems to solve:

- How do we turn a higher percentage of the solar energy hitting the surface of a smaller, thinner solar panel into enough electricity to power an entire building? A school? A city? We must do better than today's 14 percent efficiency.

- What materials will yield the highest efficiency at an acceptable cost?

- How do we pack that capability into the thinnest solar films that will be resilient enough to stand atop buildings for decades?

These are questions for present and future engineers and scientists to answer.

Luis faces an additional hurdle in serving school districts. The least expensive solar panels—the most widely available—are the least efficient and the heaviest. We cannot put heavy solar panels on school rooftops that weren't engineered to carry additional loads. Also, will the panels be able to withstand winds and other pressures? The answer may lie in thinner panels, which are currently too expensive. Therefore, Luis' challenge is to balance cost with efficiency. However, because he is putting the business and project plan together, and not engineering new types of solar cells, he is first concerned with positioning the solution he envisions for the school district's decision makers.

Luis has a degree in accounting, plus he has broad business experience. This industry needs people like Luis who can put the pieces together and make it work. It needs people who can:

• Crunch the numbers to understand project costs and economic benefits

• Establish relationships with many subcontractors and know the unique offerings of each approach

• Create financing packages for clients to help them pay for the project

• Analyze, design, propose, source, install and maintain the components of a complete solar solution

Luis can do all of that to sell the solution. He can present it in a way which causes decision makers to act and hire him to do the work.

"At school board meetings I present the business plan. I simply say we are offering an opportunity for the district to participate in the available green technology that is powering our nation. We state that we will help them maximize their existing resources. We also ensure that decision makers understand that, in adopting these technologies for their schools, they're creating an on-site opportunity for green job creation and internships."

He does not bother the school board members with the technical details. He highlights the benefits of hiring him to harness the sun as a source of power for their schools. "The sun is there every day," Luis tells them. "I say we must capture it and use it to save money in the district's operating budget. That is the fund that currently pays their utility bills. That way we can keep that money in the classrooms, for teachers, for supplies and more."

We are at the beginning of a new phase of our economic development when solar power will become widely adopted. "I believe now is the time for schools to be adopting this form of energy, to learn how it works and why it's better," Luis states. "We must ensure our kids grow up around this type of solution, a cleaner form of energy. This way, it will be a viable, familiar energy option for them as they become adults."

Luis makes an important point, "Understand that solar energy has only become economically advantageous since President Obama arrived and he worked together with Congress to create and fund the American Recovery and Reinvestment Act."

The financial incentives the federal government provides to adopt solar energy solutions have encouraged agencies to move forward to adopt newer, greener forms of energy instead of sticking with the status quo. Luis pointed out that in the first eighteen months of this marketplace, the ones who drove the market were the engineers and installers. Now, the people who control the land and land rights are running the market. This brings us to the point of understanding what Luis' company does in this dynamic marketplace of solar energy.

Evergreen Energy Solutions, LLC

Luis' newest company is Evergreen Energy Solutions, LLC. Let's see how he chose the public school system as the beneficiary of his work.

In 1994 Luis and his sister, Virginia created the Del Terra Group, a program and construction management company. Luis' company manages capital improvements like new schools, new sewers lines and other projects typically paid for with municipal bond programs.

Bond programs are financing vehicles that cities can issue to pay for improvements to buildings and infrastructure. These must be tangible improvements with long lives, not things like payroll and operating expenses.

Many years after the spreadsheet incident in Montebello that opened new doors, Luis read an article about a Northern California company offering solar energy solutions to residences. He asked himself why this opportunity to save money and be environmentally sensitive couldn't also work for schools.

"I realized I already knew the school districts, their challenges and their needs. I also knew the decision makers in my districts," Luis shares. "I knew I wanted to stay in the school business, to help them out because they need so much assistance. It was the next natural step in what I could offer."

He understood the need to reduce expenses paid through the schools' operating funds. This became more important to his clients as the California budget crisis deepened. Luis started doing energy audits of schools and began to suggest newer equipment that used less energy. He provided estimates on the megawatts of consumption and costs that could be reduced if they took a different path. Luis wanted to help our schools save money while doing something good for the community.

In 2009 Luis launched Evergreen Energy Solutions, LLC, of which he is the President and CEO. The company is 100 percent Latino-owned (an important designation to compete for government contracts), certified by the California Energy Commission and a full-service solar technology developer. It provides solar energy to public agencies such as school districts, municipalities and utility agencies. The company helps clients reduce their carbon footprints, converting the electrical needs of their facilities (school buildings, administration buildings, computer and science lab buildings, gymnasiums, city halls, utility generating plants, libraries, etc.) to solar energy. Evergreen provides all the necessary engineering, panels, installation, maintenance and operation of solar energy systems. It can also facilitate complete project financing. [Source: Congressional Hispanic Caucus Institute handout "*Latinos Leading in the Green Economy*"]

Luis points out that when working on bond-funded projects, they must be specified completely before the work begins. Changes along the way result in costly fines. Therefore, this type of work in the public sector requires skilled project management to ensure that the scope of work is planned and documented correctly up front. This requirement increases the likelihood that the project will be completed on time and within the allotted budget.

Evergreen also offers creative financing options, usually through private financing and sometimes through local utility agencies. This helps school districts offset costs without dipping into their operating funds. Sometimes power purchase agreements are involved where Evergreen provides the federal grant writing services to secure that funding. The key is that Luis knows the options, has contacts in the organizations needed to do the deal, and can crunch the numbers to make sure the economics work. That accounting degree has proven to be quite beneficial.

Luis suggests a variety of ideas to his clients. Panels can be installed in parking lots to capture and convert sunlight while also shading cars from the heat of the day. They can also be installed over areas where children eat, play and rest. Most of his clientele is outside Los Angeles in the surrounding cities of Hacienda Heights, La Puente, Bassett, Baldwin Park, El Monte, Whittier, Rosemead, Montebello, Lynwood and Compton.

"I have always looked where nobody else was looking," Luis states. "We are creating a whole new market. Plus, we are introducing students to the technology being implemented in their schools. We create internship opportunities directly related to the project. We cause job creation by hiring talent from the neighborhood to do the work. We are working with community colleges to create courses to train students to graduate as solar installers. They will immediately be ready to do installation work. Part of their compensation is paid for by the government through the bond funding, so everyone benefits from our approach."

Luis' firm employs the highest number of Latinos and Latinas in the industry—over 90 percent of the employee base is Latino, with an almost even ratio of men to women (60 to 40 percent). To date Luis has signed contracts and managed $2.5 billion of public funds for capital improvements. He's been approached by Chinese and European investors. There are companies that want to buy his company. There are companies that want him to use their solar panels.

"I'm a solar developer," Luis explains. "I put the deal together. I've got engineers and installers. I go find the product that matches the specifications put forward by the client. I sub-contract the installation job. It's like a real estate development project, but slightly different."

Luis summarizes his firm's key offering, saying, "My main offering is the ability to understand the client base. I know I'm not working with an empty building. My client has school in session. There are young children around. We must know how to do the work without ever disrupting the curriculum. This takes conscientious planning and meticulous timing. We understand these factors. We understand the need for safety, for background checks of the contractors (to be cleared to work on campus) and other such requirements. Project management is always part of it. It's one of our strengths. People hire us for our expertise in serving school districts and our planning and execution services."

In early 2011, Luis had five different school districts signed up for his energy solutions. "I have a captive market," he says. "It has been a natural segue to energy efficiency from the projects I was already managing for these school district clients."

According to the California Department of Education District Organization Handbook, there are 963 school districts in the state. According to the U. S. Census Bureau, there are over 15,000 school districts in the nation. You can see that Luis, and other solar developers who will certainly follow, have a huge market to tap.

There is a lot of work to be done—and potential money to be made—by those who will lead the projects to re-power our nation's schools with solar energy and other alternative energy sources.

Motivation to Work in the Green Economy

Luis reflects on those early years working in his father's auto mechanic business. He realizes that many of his invaluable personal and professional attributes originated in his father's shop: self-confidence, a strong work ethic, creativity in problem-solving and knowing how to manage a profitable business. Of course, during those years Luis didn't actually enjoy being there with his dad; he would have much rather spent his time playing with friends. Today, Luis looks back at those years with gratitude and a sense of good fortune. They formed the foundation of the dedication and energy with which he approaches today's business endeavors. Luis was able to witness the many real-world challenges that his father had to handle.

I asked Luis about his motivation to work in the green economy and to make solar energy solutions a reality for our public schools.

"My family is my motivation. I have three kids. Having the ability to continue on is important. I see the way we are using our natural resources is not very good. The oil spill, the coal we consume, etc. My kids are only six, four and two years old. I have to do my part. My kids will be able to see that I tried to improve the world for them in a very real way. I have a strong goal to preserve the world, to use this energy wisely. Introducing solar solutions into the school environment is one way to do it. But I also know from my years in business that whatever I do must be economically beneficial to my clients, or it won't happen."

Luis has found the place where economics meets sustainable practices, where embracing cleaner forms of energy results in real savings (in this case lower utility bills for schools). That's where adoption will happen. Luis' focused approach, and the creativity he brings to the design and management of such a project, offers the nation a best practice to emulate. Think globally, act locally. As word gets out to other school districts about how Luis' first clients are saving chunks of money from their operating budgets while exposing their students to greener, cleaner energy technologies, more districts will surely follow and start their own solar projects. Certainly, as Evergreen Energy Solutions rolls out more projects and racks up more successes, it will reach new milestones.

"One of my districts is thinking very ambitiously," he shares. "They want to utilize solar energy to supply all *district-wide* lighting, not just one or two buildings. They want the sun to provide *all* electricity throughout all their buildings. We're almost there. We're getting the design plan done and it will be installed within the year."

Luis knows these milestones will trigger investors to put in more money, looking to see what else can be done. This will accelerate the adoption of this form of energy.

"School districts are the biggest landowners in many cities," Luis states. "School districts can therefore become examples to homeowners, showing them that the technology works on a large scale. Then homeowners can take this important step too, and make the switch to solar. Our school-aged kids will then see solar power in use every day, at home and at school. This will make solar energy a natural part of their lives. It will change the way we all think about how we generate our electricity."

Our kids will soon be asking us why we didn't do this sooner and what took us so long to wean off the dirtier forms of energy and onto the cleaner, renewable sources. The sun has always been there. Thanks to innovators and change agents like Luis, our nation will see many examples of solar energy success and many more of us will be inspired to finally make the switch.

Luis Recommends

Need help becoming more comfortable as a public speaker? Join Toastmasters International. This organization is a world leader in helping people become more competent and comfortable in front of an audience. It boasts 260,000 members in over 12,500 clubs in

113 countries. It offers a proven and fun way to practice and hone communication and leadership skills. www.toastmasters.org

ALPFA (the Association of Latino Professionals in Finance and Accounting, formerly the American Association of Hispanic CPAs that Luis mentioned in his story). www.alpfa.org

NOTE: Resources for the solar industry are listed in the chapter about Robert Zardeneta and LA CAUSA.

Resources to Learn the Science and Technology of Converting the Sun's Energy into Useful Electricity

Here are some of the best articles I read on how the sun's energy is converted into electricity.

1. An October 2008 article from *Scientific American* titled, "How does solar power work?"
www.scientificamerican.com/article.cfm?id=how-does-solar-power-work

2. The Energy Kids website is provided by the U.S. Energy Information Administration. It includes information about all energy resources, including solar. www.eia.doe.gov/kids/energy.cfm?page=solar_home-basics

If you are even more curious, read this *Scientific American* article about thin-film solar technologies to understand how using significantly fewer materials made of different compounds, at a greatly reduced cost, can ultimately convert a higher percentage of sun to electricity. "Solar Power Lightens Up with Thin-Film Technology". www.scientificamerican.com/article.cfm?id=solar-power-lightens-up-with-thin-film-cells

You may want to study this chart from the National Renewable Energy Laboratory. It charts the "Best Research-Cell Efficiencies" worldwide, with the names of universities, labs and enterprises and the efficiencies

they have achieved with a wide variety of materials and approaches.
www.nrel.gov/pv/thin_film/docs/kaz_best_research_cells.ppt

Company-owned photo by Tulio Romo

Luis with the renewable energy system he's bringing to California's public schools
www.evergreensolarsolutions.com

Sandra Artalejo

Turning Throwaways into Beautiful Fashion Accessories

*I*magine growing up watching your grandmother pour sand into four large coffee cans, seal and upholster them, creating a footrest for your grandfather. What lessons about conservation and reuse might you take away and apply in your professional life as an adult? Meet the woman who frequently stayed with her grandparents, watching them create jewelry out of stale bread dough and still-life art out of whatever seeds, flowers and twigs nature had to offer.

Sandra Artalejo is a Dallas-based fashion designer whose work includes the Selena Junior and Girls line inspired by the late Tejano music star, Selena Quintanilla. She has merged her fashion design expertise and her passion for art to create an eco-friendly line of fashion and lifestyle products that highlights the beauty of reuse. Give the woman a dog food bag then step back. In a short time, she will transform it into a fabulous beach tote or a funky backpack. Now that is a product you'll feel good about using or giving as a gift!

To truly understand how Sandra came to honor the second R of "Reduce, Reuse, Recycle," with such creativity, we must first meet Sandra's grandparents and parents. Young Sandra spent many weekends at her grandparents' home in El Paso, Texas. It was a creativity-rich, loving environment, where reuse was the norm; very little was thrown away.

Sandra tells us her grandparents said, "We don't waste anything. If we get something, we use it. Then we figure out how to use it for other purposes."

Why buy a can to mix paint in when you can use a coffee can? Why buy wrapping paper when you can use a newspaper?

Her grandmother was a seamstress, always creating something new for herself or family members to wear. She created original designs for her customers, using newspapers to make patterns. Wedding gowns, dresses, formal wear and men's suits were just some of the garments she created. Her grandfather worked on the railroad, but his passion was art. He was an incredible painter and sculptor. He creatively reused many found things.

Sandra remembers, "He would put leftover bread crumbs in the coffee can and call it a bird feeder. The birds waited for this feast daily. Nothing was wasted."

"It was a treat to spend the night at their house because there was so much going on all the time. I remember so distinctly the warm, soft color and uniquely creaky sound of the hardwood floors. In my mind, I see my *abuelito* rolling his cigarettes and I remember the strong scent of tobacco. I loved watching him paint as my *abuelita* was sewing. I wanted to be just like them."

Of the constant reuse activity she witnessed, Sandra says, "As a child, I perceived it purely as creativity in my grandparents and parents."

Her mother, like many mothers of Mexican descent, made clothes for the children at home. Sandra says, "My mom made all our clothes—her mom had made all of her clothes. She made curtains and bedspreads too. If she could have made our shoes, she would have done so."

Sandra's mother skillfully cut and twisted aluminum cans into daisies, roses and other flower shapes. She placed them around the garden as shiny accents. She created artistic items from milk and egg cartons. "Is it any wonder that now I am using aluminum cans to create fashionable headbands?" Sandra asks.

Sandra's father was a very talented sketch artist, something she discovered when she came across a sketch of her mother. "I was completely blown away by it," she recalls.

Career and School Choices

When asked about her career choices as a young woman, Sandra shared, "Because my mom sewed, I wanted to go into fashion design to see what I could create. I wanted to make a living doing this."

Sandra tried other jobs. "I worked in a bank and in an office, but I did not enjoy it. It was really boring. I needed something creative to do." When I asked why she did not like office jobs, she replied, "I felt like I was a scribble of color in a grey, straight-line world." This answer reveals much about Sandra's life choices.

Many believe they must go to New York City or Los Angeles to be a fashion designer. Sandra knew she wanted a four-year degree and that she wanted to stay in Texas. She chose the University of the Incarnate Word, a Catholic university in San Antonio.

"It was a cool school and fit my cultural values and upbringing," she explains. "The campus is gorgeous, with old churches, history and plenty of nuns. I always thought nuns were cool."

Sandra explains that her school was a "funky," wonderful place, rich with history. The head of the fashion design department was a worldly Irish nun who loved to sew.

"She was one of the most difficult instructors I had, but she taught me so much," Sandra reflects. "She was the opposite of conservative. She encouraged us to go wild in our designs; she encouraged us to push the creative envelope."

The nun commented one day about Sandra's Catholic jewelry. She said she was happy to see her display her beliefs and faith so openly. Sandra recalls responding with, "Catholicism is the religion that has the coolest accessories. Why wouldn't I wear them?" She loved wearing her rosaries to class—long before pop star Madonna did so.

Learning fashion design from an Irish nun in San Antonio is certainly an unusual path into the glamorous world of fashion. This decision represents the different perspective Sandra would bring into the fashion design industry after completing her bachelor degree.

• BS in fashion design, University of the Incarnate Word

A Peek into the Fashion Design World

Many people think fashion design is about unapproachable designers creating outrageous designs that most people will never wear. To enter the fashion design industry, most people study fashion design in school, then hopefully find an apprenticeship in the industry. Sandra's early perception was that most of the couture designers were truly out of touch with the real public. She noted that original designs are typically changed, simplified and finally trickle down to mainstream retail for mass production and consumption.

Throughout her fashion design career, Sandra took clothing lines from initial illustrations through product development. She worked with buying and technical teams throughout the development process. She has used her marketing and merchandising skills in Europe, New York and Los Angeles to research and prepare for developing trends.

I asked how Sandra came to create the line of clothes with Selena Quintanilla's name on it.

"I was working for a clothing manufacturer in Dallas at the time of Selena's tragic death," she explains. "The Selena movie was created soon after she died. One of the sponsors was JCPenney®. At the time, I was designing lines for them. They indicated to my employer their interest in carrying a line in their stores with Selena's name. I sketched some ideas, was flown to meet the Quintanilla family, and started the Selena line working with Suzette Quintanilla. The clothing line was something Selena had wanted—Suzette fulfilled her dream."

Sandra confesses, "Throughout my career, I loved the designing part, but the superficial part bothered me. I am talking about the image stuff, that idea that you must wear a certain thing a certain way and be rail-thin and super-young to be beautiful."

The fashion industry attitude bothered her. "I noticed the cliques. I'm sure most workplaces have them, but there seemed to be distinct separations," she recalls. "I worked with everyone and respected everyone. I remembered my grandmother as I saw the seamstresses, working late into the night, finishing garments for people who really did not pay much. I saw her in the Latinas who were sewing for the designers. I loved them; they were wonderful, strong women who took so much pride in their work. I loved eating lunch with them and getting to know them as people, not just as seamstresses."

Sandra also reveals her disappointment that the fashion industry is extremely wasteful. She describes a common scene. "I would go see where the cuts were being done. The pattern of the garment would be cut out and the rest of the fabric thrown away. Sometimes the dumpster in the back would be overflowing with scraps. My grandmother and mother would have had a fit! They would have been able to make a quilt, pillows—so many things out of these scraps. Where was it going to go? To the landfill—hundreds of pounds of fabric in the dumpster every day were such a waste. It really bothered me."

Could a woman who grew up watching grandma create clothes, quilts and so many more useful household items out of fabric remnants ignore such wasteful acts?

Sandra tells us, "Fashion is such an image-based industry. Unless it's cool, new and the latest trend, it's not salable. It's a very fickle industry. That's another reason why the industry is not much into being green. Only if someone famous starts acting and becoming 'green,' then those in the industry will jump on the bandwagon." It's hard to be a maverick and create "green" fashion when it's not perceived as a cool thing.

Eventually, Sandra could no longer ignore the fabric in the dumpsters. She despised the waste and the attitude and began to lean more toward art. And so began Sandra's intentional combining of art and fashion through creative reuse.

"What I do is not fashion for fashion's sake. These pieces have a purpose. I want to take the snob appeal out of it. I want the main reason for my work to be an example of reuse." It's a perfect trio—art, fashion and reuse—all coming together in her uniquely fashionable way. I asked what trends she sees in the industry—is it becoming more responsible and green in any way?

"I have not seen a gamut of couture fashion designers creating 'green' fashion, but I do have hope. The waste I have seen is still happening," Sandra answers. "This industry will be a hard one to crack, but the smaller designers and design houses are the ones that are making the changes in the industry."

What about the so-called "green fabrics" and natural clothes being touted today? She explains, "Yes, there are lots of green fabrics created from bamboo and organic cotton, but they are all *new* materials. There is no reuse there. It's a very different thing when you are taking something that exists and will be thrown away, and instead give it a second life." Even so, she believes those companies using more natural materials should be commended. They are on the green path in their own way. She feels that, even though the natural fabric trend is growing, reuse and redesign is a bit more challenging.

Sandra's Entrepreneurial Approach

In early 2000, Sandra began to seriously experiment with creating new designs with used objects. Her first designs were headbands and wristbands made of recycled candy wrappers, and totes made of recycled dog food bags. She created her company, Sola Studios, in 2006. Sola Studios specializes in freelance and consulting in fashion design, illustration, and product sourcing and development.

Sandra's designs have included a contemporary women's wear line, fashions for young Latina women, lingerie and sleepwear, loungewear, children's wear, work wear, western wear, handbags, hair accessories and jewelry. She has also created treatments for tabletops, beds, baths and windows. The line of products she created is called AMP Accessories, which stands for Art, Music and Purpose. She also has created a gift line of bookmarks, purses, headbands, wristbands and other products that give new life to items that already have served their first purpose.

Luckily, Sandra has plenty of storage space in her studio for her raw materials—wine boxes, Pop-Tart® boxes, potato chip bags, bottle caps, candy wrappers, aluminum cans, vinyl records, wallpaper samples and recycled bottles. She admits she cannot throw most things away. She finds an abundance of something being wasted and finds a way to keep it out of the landfill by redesigning it. It may take some time and multiple prototypes to achieve the desired function, but she eventually figures it out.

"In my bedroom I have these beautiful wine boxes. Some have dragons or swans on the cover. I put paper in them to make journals. I made a Pop-Tart box into a note pad. I made a clutch out of dog food bags. For a swim party for one of my daughter's friends, I made my first beach bag out of dog food bags. I was throwing them away, but they were so strong. I had to figure out how to make them into something else."

In her studio, raw materials are organized and ready for reuse. Everything is categorized so she can find whatever she needs quickly and easily. Her commitment to turn one person's throwaway into another person's treasure has attracted positive press in the Dallas community. From that, more opportunities for new materials and new designs have surfaced. As a result of a 2009 *Dallas News* article, she was contacted by a local business that makes billboards.

"I have developed a line from their discarded material that I would like to present to businesses interested in recycled accessories," she shares. "I admire this local billboard company and believe they are paving the way for other businesses to step up and rethink what they are throwing away. They are determined to find a way to create something new instead. They are thinking outside the box."

Think about the positive environmental impact that could happen if every corporation printing billboards, trade show banners and the like had those items redesigned into tote bags (or other giveaways) for subsequent events. Remember the billboard banners Carmen's company is printing that should be recycled but instead are sent to the landfill? What if Carmen's clients' banners made their way to Sandra for creative reuse? Think of the resources that could be spared if this type of reuse became the norm. Think of the serious uptick in a corporation's green credentials if they could promote this reuse practice. Their competitors could choose to follow their example, amplifying the positive resource reuse impact.

Sandra's Motivation

In the 2009 interview, Sandra said, "Recycling and reusing is something I am working on with my daughter. She has truly inspired me to create more products and perhaps make an impression on a whole new generation."

Sandra has involved her teenage daughter, Francesca, in the actual creative process of designing through reusing. More importantly, her daughter and her friends have full awareness of Sandra's passion to create using existing raw materials; they think the results are cool. These teens have accepted this entire process as fashionable and hip. They offer ideas back to Sandra for new creations.

"My daughter is my tester—she's my target market. I get feedback from her and her friends. They like things made of brightly colored candy wrapper bags. She comes home with dozens of bags and says, "Look, Mom. Here are some cool potato chip bags and more candy bags."

Imagine Francesca's attitude becoming the norm among America's teenagers. How might that transform their thinking about resources and reduce their need to consume over a lifetime?

Sandra says, "If you go to the malls, you see so-called designer jeans that are shredded, ripped and painted. They cost $90." Sandra and Francesca went to the thrift store and picked up well-worn jeans, ripped them, dripped some paint on them and reproduced the $90 jeans for five dollars a pair. Clearly, the creative reuse torch has been passed. Yet, there are some serious challenges to taking this creative reuse idea to mainstream society. The biggest challenge Sandra has encountered so far are short-sighted adults who create obstacles.

"Francesca got very involved in the eco movement long ago. A teacher of hers tried to start a recycling club to teach these ideas at school," Sandra tells us. Her daughter had spread the word at school about creative reuse. She took headbands, bookmarks and other samples to school and the kids were excited. They collected chip bags and other items from the cafeteria to start. Then suddenly it all stopped. "I was told it wasn't endorsed by the administration. I was told that a recycling and reusing club wasn't on the list of approved clubs you can have at school."

Francesca and her friends were deeply disappointed. Sandra approached a city recycling official with her idea to collect reusable materials at schools.

"I volunteered to teach kids how to make new things out of used things," she explains. "I suggested the school could sell the items we made and take a percentage of sales as a fundraiser. The official said he had no idea who would want to make or buy these things. I was totally shocked...no foresight...wow."

Sandra and Francesca will eventually find a way to go around these small thinkers and make a significant difference in their community. Kids will benefit with new, creative skills and schools will benefit with revenue. For now, Sandra is happy to be keeping things from ever making it to the landfill, while helping companies turn expensive mistakes into something valuable to the community.

"I have approached companies that have misprinted bags. I can change their trash into cash; into something that is worth something to someone else," she says. "In this process, many new people learn to reuse and recycle. If we repeat this cycle with our young kids, we can teach them that materials used in packaging can become something else."

The Accolades

Sandra's innovative design work has repeatedly received recognition. Early on, at the Hispanic Designer Gala in Washington, D.C., she was recognized as a "Rising Star." The Texas Presswomen presented her with a First Place Graphics Award. The National Presswomen did the same. She won a LULAC (League of United Latin American Citizens) Hispanic Entrepreneur National Award. She was named the Hispanic Designer of the Year and received the Catwalk Award in Dallas. Recently, CHCI (the Congressional Hispanic Caucus Institute) recognized Sandra as a leader in our green economy.

One of Sandra's art pieces was recently chosen for the La Reunion Natural Artist installations. Her piece was called "*La Reina de La Reunion*," and she made it entirely of seeds, twigs and other items found in nature. The idea was to create a temporary piece of art that would go entirely back into the earth. [See photos of this beautiful piece that has since biodegraded at www.latinnovating.com]

Clearly, Sandra is onto something—a new way to innovate, redesign and reuse, while creating beautiful, fashionable items for personal use and for gifting. She is a true *latinnovator*.

Sandra's Vision of Fashion, Art and Reuse Possibilities

"I love the idea of permanence from the disposable," says Sandra.

It's a profound thought. Why not come up with a permanently useful function for something you will otherwise throw away? Have you ever made cut-off shorts from an old pair of jeans? Why not turn the remaining denim into a couple of purses for little girls? There are endless reuse examples of "permanence from the disposable."

"My vision is that we stop being a throwaway society—not just the kids in art classes," Sandra says. She believes that creative reuse must be taught to millions of people. An entirely new industry can be created where raw materials are nearly free because they would otherwise be thrown away.

Sandra explains, "We could create new jobs in the United States reusing these readily-available materials. We could teach people how to make objects that are commonly needed by consumers and businesses. We'd just make them from existing materials. We could have collection barrels, as common as trash cans, where people could drop off used product, wrapping, whatever. These would be taken to factories in the United States, where new jobs would be created specifically for manufacturing reused, redesigned products. These products, in turn, would be sold for consumption and more capital would be pumped into our economy. Everybody wins."

New business models must be created to make Sandra's vision a reality. Someone just needs to recognize the potential, think it through and lead the execution. Who will take her ideas and build upon them?

Sandra has taught courses in fashion illustration, textiles, portfolio and fashion show production. She sees that very few teach the art of reuse through redesign.

A movie contributed to Sandra's passion. "When I saw the *Mad Max* movies, I thought they were so cool! They were reusing everything because they were trying to survive. They *had* to reuse. So when our world is dying, who is going to survive? The creative people— that is who is going to survive." Those are chilling words, given the *Mad Max* movies.

Sandra Recommends

For high school students interested in exploring careers in fashion design, Sandra recommends that you get ideas for new fashion from all walks of life—inspiration can come from anywhere. Study what people are wearing at the airport, the theater, the opera and the mall. Look for universities, art institutes or community colleges that offer fashion design and get a four-year degree. Learn how to sew and draw; learn about different types of materials. Don't believe that certain people must wear certain types of clothes. Understand that people's individual personalities inspire their choice of clothes. You can't stereotype what people want.

See examples of Sandra's fashion design work and the products in the AMP Accessories line at www.solastudios.net.

For college students, Sandra offers: "Be sure you have some business skills so you can understand the elements of production costs, accounting and marketing tactics. If you are studying fashion or art already, start looking for objects that people are throwing away. Check out fabric stores and hardware stores, and look for things that are available in large quantities and free. Examples are keys at hardware stores. When they are bad cuts, they get put into a box and then returned to the manufacturer, causing additional transportation expense and waste. Instead, I made a cool jacket with 300 keys. You just need to ask for the 'bad cuts.' They can also be made into bookmarks."

For those in mid-career transition into something more creative, she suggests you find continued education classes in fashion sketching, design or art to see how you like it. From there, decide what areas are the best fit for you.

Additional Recommendations

Read the article titled "Dallas artist finds unusual beauty in discarded items," www.dallasnews.com/sharedcontent/dws/fea/greenliving/stories/DN-nhm_green_1128gd.ART.State.Edition1.1b94e10.html.

Find ideas on alternatives for gift wrapping paper at "Green living: Wrap packages cheaply with found items," www.dallasnews.com/sharedcontent/dws/fea/home/howto/stories/DN-nhm_green_1219gd.ART.State.Edition1.b1d080.html.

Learn about the "funky, coolest ever" Catholic university Sandra attended. Visit www.uiw.edu.

Visit this online store that features artist-designed, handmade, fashion items and things for use in the home: www.etsy.com

National Resources Defense Council: The NRDC works to protect wildlife and wild places and to ensure a healthy environment for all life on earth. Learn more at www.nrdc.org.

Company-owned photo by Lindsay M. Baker

Sandra shows the beauty of permanence from the disposable—a journal made from a wine box. www.solastudios.net

Dennis Salazar
Leading the Sustainable Packaging Industry

*H*ave you ever opened a package shipped to your home and felt completely disgusted at the amount of waste created to package and ship your small item? If so, you will appreciate the ability and the action of one man in the packaging industry who questioned these environmentally-unsound practices. He has put tremendous effort into changing these and other industry practices and encourages others to join him. The changes he's causing and promoting are the future of the packaging industry, an industry which has lagged behind many others in changing its internal processes toward sustainability.

Dennis Salazar's *abuelita* (grandmother) Juanita grew up as a migrant farm worker living in a shack. Although they had dirt floors, she diligently swept them out daily. One of her favorite sayings was "*No tenemos mucho, pero lo que tenemos está limpio y en orden.*" Translation: "We don't have much, but what we have is clean and organized."

This *dicho* instilled in Dennis a strong desire to preserve and protect what material possessions he had. This entrepreneur has made his grandmother's words a cornerstone of his business. Salazar Packaging, an innovative leader in the sustainable packaging industry, recently delivered to the market the Globe Guard® Reusable Box, the first shipping box specifically designed for reuse.

His mother grew up in a poor, small Texas town. His father arrived there from Mexico ready and eager to work.

"He came over and scraped," Dennis says. "He worked as a pourer in a foundry for over thirty years. That is the guy you see in pictures who is handling a large vat of molten steel and manually pouring the steel into a mold to make castings. That is some seriously hard work."

Dennis grew up in suburban Chicago. "We were probably better off than many," Dennis says. "We had cousins who grew up in the inner city and others living in migrant worker camps. By comparison, you could say we were comfortable in our lower-middle class environment. But we were frugal."

Because of his extended family's experiences and his parent's life experiences, Dennis always had awareness that things cost money. That money had cost someone his or her time and labor. Therefore, acquired things needed to be used wisely. His parents taught the family to save everything because of their economic reality—not out of a conservation mentality. He sees the parallel of this practice today, working with businesses of all sizes.

Dennis observes, "There are many companies today on the green bandwagon that aren't trying to save the planet—they are trying to save money. I have learned not to question their motives as long as they are changing their business processes and products to truly conserve our resources."

On-the-Job Education
When I asked Dennis about his education and training, he did not hesitate. "I am an uneducated genius. My family circumstances did not enable me to pursue formal education, yet I have tested above the 98th percentile on IQ tests. I have also served as a membership officer for the Chicago area chapter of American Mensa®."

Mensa is an international society with only one qualification: members must score in the top two percent of the general population on a standardized intelligence test. [Source: American Mensa]

Dennis received his education working within the packaging industry. He took every training class offered.

"I fortunately worked for companies that offered training and education," Dennis shares. "I received sales training and people management training. I took classes on how to motivate and discipline employees. I got training in operational processes, inventory management and supply chain management. I took courses to understand how buying and selling determine profitability. I took strategic planning courses to understand where I wanted to go and how I was going to get there."

This abundance of training eventually resulted in a promotion to Regional Vice President of the packaging systems group at Unisource®, when the company was a $7 billion-a-year global enterprise. He was the youngest and only Latino Regional VP in the company. He is laser-focused and educated, in a dynamic, evolving industry that has held his attention for decades. If only the rest of America's employees could be so fortunate.

• Abundant corporate training and education within his industry

Questioning the Status Quo

Dennis met his wife Lenora in the packaging industry. "Lenora and I realized we were part of an industry that was seen by the green community as a villain and one of the greatest polluters of the planet," he says.

Packaging products are designed to be used once and thrown away, a practice condemned by environmental groups. Typical throwaway products include corrugated cardboard boxes, thick mailing envelopes for CDs and DVDs, Styrofoam® peanuts, packing tape and cardboard tubes. Those who do recycle packaging may not recognize that the natural resources and energy needed to manufacture and transport these items have already been consumed. This resource cost could be cut in half if each item would be used twice instead of once.

The problem is that the largest buyers and users of packaging goods do not want to reuse containers because of how they look. They believe their customers want to receive items in brand new boxes and containers. Is this an accurate perception? If you ordered a book from Amazon.com, would you somehow think less of Amazon® or its Marketplace booksellers, if they sent your book in a pre-used box? How would Amazon's supply chain apply the idea of shipping items with reused boxes? Would this add to or reduce the shipping cost you pay each time you place an order?

Dennis began asking himself these types of questions. He understood after years in the industry that numerous accepted practices were generally vilified by many outsiders—and rightly so. Even as the use of recycled content packaging became more popular and the green packaging market began to grow, Dennis was bothered by the response of some bandwagon-jumping manufacturers. These companies opted to add some token amount of recycled content to their products so they could make a green claim. He expressed his belief that these products should be aiming for eighty percent or more recycled content—ideally PCW (post-consumer waste)—to legitimately be considered eco-friendly. Some of his colleagues scoffed and answered with, "Who would care? Besides, if the PCW content is too high, people will start to question the quality and performance of the product."

Dennis would encounter this attitude repeatedly within the industry. The belief was that the market didn't want or need more than just a token percentage of PCW-recycled content. The products didn't need to actually be eco-friendly. They only needed enough recycled content so that vendors could market them as being green. Using that logic, the truly sustainable corrugated cardboard box, made of 100 percent PCW recycled content, didn't exist because it didn't need to exist. And if it did exist, some said its quality would be questioned. Answers like these didn't sit well with Dennis, but they provided much-needed insight into what action he needed to take.

Dennis also adds, "The industry does not deserve all of the blame it receives. But Lenora and I both believed enough of it to be true that we had to help lead the industry to become part of the solution, rather than remain a major contributor to the problem."

By 2006, he had already started three packaging divisions for others. "I decided that before I died, I wanted to have my own packaging company. I called on my expertise and my network in the industry. Lenora and I inventoried our combined strengths, experience and skills and decided the time was right to make the change," he says.

Lenora says, "We had more than enough experience and confidence in each other to take this tremendous leap in faith. We also saw an opportunity to make a difference in what was then the emerging sustainable packaging movement."

Carving Their Own Sustainable Path

According to Global Industry Analysts (GIA), the global market for sustainable packaging is projected to reach $143 billion by 2015. In their publication titled *Sustainable (Green) Packaging: A Global Strategic Business Report*, Europe and the United States represent the largest regions for sustainable packaging, together accounting for more than seventy percent of the global market. [Source: www.environmentalleader.com/2010/08/12/global-sustainable-packaging-market-to-reach-nearly-142b-by-2015]

Another group, Pike Research, indicates that the sustainable packaging market is growing much faster than the overall packaging industry. It is expected to double in size from $88 billion in 2009 to $170 billion in 2014. [Source: www.environmentalleader.com/2010/01/05/pike-research-finds-global-sustainable-packaging-market-to-double-by-2014]

The time was right for the Salazars to grab their piece of a very big pie. In 2007, with their combined forty-plus years of packaging industry experience, Lenora and Dennis walked away from their comfortable, professional salaries and started Salazar Packaging, Inc. They had such deep commitment to sustainable business practices and the environment that they left their corporate careers that were providing nice salaries to enjoy life and travel at their leisure. Few people in their situation would seriously consider leaving a cushy lifestyle behind to start a business from scratch, with all the risk, uncertainty and discomfort that typically accompanies such a dramatic change. Dennis and Lenora are truly environmental entrepreneurs.

Their minimal personal debt enabled them to fund the company on their own. They immediately focused on rounding up truly green products to offer to their customers. For example, they turned their backs on low, token-recycled content boxes in favor of 100 percent PCW boxes. Where they saw a lack of solutions for customers demanding actual green solutions (instead of solutions based on "greenwashing" claims), they created their own innovative products.

The sustainable packaging industry is still relatively young. The Sustainable Packaging Coalition (SPC) is an industry working group striving to meet today's market needs without harming others in the future. This is their definition of sustainable packaging:

Sustainable packaging:

• Is beneficial, safe and healthy for individuals and communities throughout its life cycle

• Meets market criteria for both performance and cost

• Is sourced, manufactured, transported and recycled using renewable energy

• Optimizes the use of renewable or recycled source materials

• Is manufactured using clean production technologies and best practices

• Is made from materials healthy in all probable end-of-life scenarios

• Is physically designed to optimize materials and energy

• Is effectively recovered and utilized in biological and/or industrial closed loop cycles

Source: The Sustainable Packaging Coalition

Dennis summarizes the vision of the sustainable packaging industry this way: "Delivering products and processes to businesses interested in reducing their carbon footprint, optimizing labor and operational costs versus what they've done historically."

Because the industry is new, he feels called upon to educate customers about what is possible and available. Decision makers cannot make better decisions for their supply chain if they don't know what is available. They need alternatives to the status quo. Dennis explains, "We are creating and helping to transform our industry daily. I like to think we've changed some minds as we've increased our exposure. We've exerted thought leadership as well as market and product design oriented leadership. It's very gratifying."

Dennis has had excellent intuition about what it takes to run a small and growing business in a fast-growing industry. He has approached this venture as an opportunity to become a thought leader, and to change the minds of peers and colleagues with non-sustainable beliefs and perceptions about sustainability.

When Salazar Packaging opened, it immediately focused on providing eco-friendly, sustainable packaging products and solutions. Dennis reflects on the immediate balancing act they faced, "It was challenging to innovate and influence within a packaging industry that assumed—and in some quarters even hoped—that sustainability was merely another passing fad. At the same time, we had to satisfy the requirements of a skeptical green community who accused our industry of being the primary violator of the planet, and understandably questioned our every claim."

The Salazars had colleagues and peers within the industry telling them not to put too much stock into going green. These people truly believed the sustainability movement was a fad and questioned the Salazars' commitment and desire to improve long-standing processes. When they tried to communicate actual, verifiable improvements in sustainable practices, they were faced with groups of skeptical environmentalists. However, the Salazars have been able to exert considerable influence inside and outside the industry. Finding this balance is part of what has made Salazar Packaging a successful innovator and thought leader in such a short time.

One reason for this success has been their desire for "sustainable authenticity and transparency" about their products and claims. "We help make green companies greener," is something Dennis says frequently at presentations. How are they doing this? Let's look at the innovations the Salazars have delivered.

First, they addressed the specific challenges they heard from eco-friendly business buyers who wanted to ship products to like-minded customers:

• "Eco-friendly packaging products are not available."

• "The minimums are ridiculously high."

• "The lead times are long."

• "The pricing is outrageous."

Salazar Packaging has consistently raised the bar in sustainable packaging by creating several new products. They created the Globe Guard® brand and an e-commerce green packaging store. The Globe Guard brand is described as "the industry's first green packaging brand that transcends product." The brand is put only on "authentically green packaging products" such as a line of 100 percent PCW recycled content corrugated shipping boxes. They put the brand on a wide variety of products that are manufactured by various industry-leading companies. Dennis says that first-time visitors are surprised to discover their prices are often lower than some national packaging distributors. They are located online at www.globeguardproducts.com.

That new idea solves a long-standing problem. Dennis and Lenora had created a reasonably priced brand name that green businesses can trust to be authentically green, a true business benefit their environmentally-conscious customers appreciate. Additionally, they're achieving true sustainable authenticity in developing their own green packaging brand. "The Globe Guard brand honestly, openly and clearly communicates the greenest approach combined with years of packaging industry knowledge," Dennis states. "It has enabled us to become a trusted supplier partner to countless green companies and green consumers."

The Globe Guard brand ensures it is the real deal. Token recycled content was never good enough for Dennis when he worked for others; it is certainly not good enough for the brand he has created. The Globe Guard designation means that a package's relative greenness is openly communicated; a customer can choose from green, greener or greenest options. Once they created the brand, they tapped their industry network to round up the greenest products with the highest recycled content. Some other manufacturers sell only the items they manufacture. Salazar Packaging has created the Globe Guard green packaging e-commerce store to serve the green market with a "one stop shop" for all of the same shipping products they can find elsewhere, at a lower cost and in a greener design and structure. Even their shipping labels are 100 percent PCW recycled content.

Their product development efforts have begun to pay off. Salazar has a patent pending on a Globe Guard Reusable Box. This first-of-its-kind box enables companies to reduce costs by quickly and easily permitting the multiple uses of a single shipping box.

Why is this innovation so important? The vast majority of cardboard boxes are used only once then discarded. They are not structurally weakened or physically destroyed, it is just that they *look* like used boxes. Therefore, Dennis invented a box that can easily be inverted and resealed to look like a brand new box in a matter of seconds. Its sheer and simple brilliance is a true resource-saving idea. *Packaging Design* Magazine called the Globe Guard Reusable Box a "dramatic step forward in reusable packaging." See a video of this innovation at www.reusableshippingboxes.com.

Dennis notes, "We are helping to bring the packaging industry and the green community together with our writing, our speaking and our innovative products. Our work has helped key manufacturers create and produce more eco-friendly products. We have also helped the green community to understand why it is important that they use these products whenever possible. We have been instrumental in changing inaccurate mindsets like the outdated perception that maintains that green packaging products do not perform well and are more expensive. We help green companies deliver a greener image and save money in the process. That has captured enough attention to make a difference."

Dennis has written many articles and blog entries. He is a true thought leader and an excellent writer. He has found a way to exert even more influence and to continuously prove his ability to see opportunities outside the box—literally. He has published articles about sustainability initiatives and organizational behavior.

I highly recommend reading his article entitled, "Is There a Disconnect In Your Green Company?" Located online at www.green biz.com/blog/2009/02/17/there-disconnect-your-green-company.

In this piece, Dennis provides expert analysis on why a C-level executive can describe the company's sustainability initiatives in detail yet the shipping clerk in that same company has no idea the company has these initiatives. If the clerk has not heard of these initiatives, he probably is not complying with them. Dennis describes the reasons middle managers do not buy into corporate sustainability initiatives, and tell their subordinates to "just wait a few months and management will move on to something else." His expertise in coaching at enterprises of all sizes, and employees at all levels, is evident in his writing. His articles should be required reading for all employees of companies who have, or want to have, sustainability programs in place. These articles expose flawed ways of approaching the concept that are surely repeated daily by managers lacking Dennis' insight.

Dennis proudly states, "Our customers include some of the largest and oldest green companies, as well as eco-conscious startups launching and operating from their kitchen tables."

Dennis also penned an article published on the "Sustainable is Good" site exposing the U.S. Post Office's practices and policies that are not sustainable. He informs us that it is against USPS regulations to reuse a box. He writes, "You would think that a service provider expected to lose over $3 billion this year would be interested in minimizing wasted packaging, if not for green's sake, for economic good sense." He also reveals the truth about the post office's white Priority Mail envelopes and boxes which contain all-new (not recycled) material. One of America's largest government agencies is perpetuating unsustainable practices.

Dennis likes to expose the green pretenders, who deceptively promote themselves as being green. This is an important service Dennis is providing to get more people to truly reflect on what practices are sustainable, environmentally-sound improvements, and which practices we must outwardly reject. One recent blog post featured an encounter with an "eco-friendly, reusable green bag" at a trade show. It screamed "Made of 80% post-consumer waste" on the outside. Later, when he dumped his bag out, he noticed, "…two small labels inside and the incredibly tiny print on them. I realized the bag was made of 100 percent polypropylene and that it was manufactured in China." Those who regularly import low-cost plastic bags state that many foreign manufacturers will gladly produce any message you want. They are not interested in the level of truthfulness. Their job is only to make products as cheaply as possible and get them to the customer in time. If you read this article, you will forever be skeptical of similar claims. Transparency and truth are important to Dennis.

Dennis is not your typical business owner. He is gifted in his intuition and in his writing. He sees things the rest of us miss. Dennis is an innovator in the truest sense of the word, a man in the right place, with the right partner, the right life experiences and the right business skills, all at the right time to really push the sustainable packaging industry in the direction it needs to go. As further proof of this, in his most recent contribution, Dennis brought together five leading U.S. distributors of sustainable packaging to launch the Green Packaging Group (www.greenpackaginggroup.com). This is the first-ever, cooperative website of business-to-business, eco-friendly packaging suppliers. Through these leading companies, buyers can find packaging products that are fully vetted and authentically sustainable. Read more about that innovation at www.prweb.com/releases/2010/08/prweb4362494.htm

Dennis is also driven to be a visible role model to our next generation of entrepreneurs. In one of the first emails I received from Dennis, he wrote:

> "As you have already figured out, I enjoy talking about my industry, business and sustainability, especially when I feel I can have a positive impact on the Latino community. By far, my favorite presentation was to a group of inner city (mostly Latino) high school students. The students participated in an after-school program called Aspira, which is designed to help encourage and develop them as potential entrepreneurs. I was invited to tell them about what we do. They were so interested in us and in sustainability. I have never had so many great questions asked after any presentation anywhere. As I fought the rush hour traffic back to the southwest suburbs where my home and business are located, all I could think about was the amazing kids I had just met and how truly blessed I was to have had the opportunity to possibly make a difference in their lives."

Throughout this book, I offer actionable steps for you to take to emulate these innovators. These steps are tied to the very reasons I wrote this book—to lift up those who have taken the risks for the greater good, to showcase those who are succeeding at their sustainability-driven ventures, and to show others the path to join them.

Dennis offered this wisdom to those entering the job market or thinking of a career transition into this emerging industry:

1. Work for a green company with true sustainability practices in place to gain crucial on-the-job-training, education and experience.

2. Consider a degree (or at least a minor) in environmental sciences or sustainability. They are becoming more available today and will look great on a resume. [Note: if you're looking at graduate school, there are now green MBA programs popping up all over the country.

Dominican University of California and the Presidio School of Management in the San Francisco Bay Area are two such examples.]

3. Take advantage of the incredible amount of information available to you on the Internet. As you read and learn, consider blogging on your own area of interest. It will help you connect with other like-minded people, including potential employers.

For Latinos, Dennis offers this bonus wisdom: "Be proud and promote your Latino heritage. Remember, the type of company that has a committed sustainability program is also likely to have a committed diversity program. We can debate whether being 'green' or 'brown' today is more important. However, the combination of the two is tough to beat."

Dennis Recommends
Dennis suggests the following resources for high school students, college students and professionals interested in the sustainable packaging industry.

To get a general background on today's sustainability trends, visit www.greenbiz.com or www.environmentalleader.com. Both are excellent websites that deliver sustainability news and perspective in the broadest sense.

Read Dennis' blog, Sustainable is Good, for an overview of sustainability trends with an emphasis on products and packaging. Find it at www.sustainableisgood.com.

For a basic foundation to learn about sustainability and packaging trends, visit Sustainable Packaging Coalition and its projects at www.sustainablepackaging.org/uploads/Documents/SPC%20 Overview.pdf

Read *Packaging Digest*, available in print and online to keep up with trends, innovations, materials and technology driving the packaging industry. This is an easy read that is free of technical jargon about processing equipment. You can find this magazine at www.packagingdigest.com.

Check out the Inside Sustainable Packaging blog from Salazar Packaging at www.blog.salazarpackaging.com. This blog has achieved acclaim in both the packaging and green communities for an open and generous sharing of cost-reducing, environmentally-beneficial techniques and ideas.

Additional Recommendations

"Is the United States Postal Service Coasting on Green?" www.sustainableisgood.com/blog/2010/01/united-states-postal-service-green.html. This is the article that exposes the U.S. Post Office's practices and policies that are clearly unsustainable. You'll want to write a letter to the U.S. Postmaster General after you read this one.

"Is Your Green Packaging Eco Obvious?" www.packagingdigest.com/blog/Common_Sense_and_Sustainability/22729-Is_Your_Green_Packaging_Eco_Obvious_.php. This article introduces the term "eco obvious"—packaging that is green in its design, content and messaging and does not require study or analysis. Read it to understand and avoid making the common mistakes made by those adopting sustainable packaging solutions.

"Am I Re-Trainable for Sustainable?" www.sustainableisgood.com/blog/2007/09/am-i-re-trainab.html. This is an excellent article for anyone who has been working for awhile in an industry or place that is not considered to be using good sustainability practices. It answers this question: What will it take for me to make the transition into the new green economy?

Just for fun: If you are wondering if you are in the top two percent of the general population as Dennis is, visit www.us.mensa.org to find out where to take the standardized intelligence test.

Dennis and Lenora show off the industry's first reversible box, designed for reuse.
www.blog.salazarpackaging.com

Humberto Rincon
Engineering a Life from One Valley to Another

The path from the fields of California's agricultural Imperial Valley to the wealth of its Silicon Valley is not a journey taken by many. Engineer Humberto Rincon is one notable exception.

The Early Years in the Hottest Valley

Humberto's parents, Eleuterio and Juana, immigrated to the United States from Mexico on Thanksgiving Day, 1963. Their Mexican-born children joined the family over the years. Eleuterio had come to work as a *bracero*, a farm laborer. Humberto was the last of nine children.

"I grew up poor in California's Imperial Valley," Humberto states. "We reused and recycled everything, because we had no choice. All containers became storage. Old tires became plant pots. All of our toys were homemade. We used newspapers and bamboo sticks to make kites using glue made of flour and water."

Make no mistake: Humberto and his siblings had great toys that they made and cherished. This way of living made the children very creative.

"The string from our flour bags became my kite string. There was about ten feet of string per bag once I pulled it off. I would tie several of these together, find a stick, wind it up and there was my kite string."

"We were always problem-solving and thinking of new uses for items," Humberto shares. "I figured out how to do things with whatever number of bottle caps I had. I figured out how to remove the cork backing from the bottle cap without breaking it. I put the cap on my shirt, reattached the cork backing from inside my shirt, and just like that I had my very own sheriff's badge. With two bottle caps, I made a hole in each and made a whistle. With four caps, I made a car. We also made our own slingshots and toy guns, as well as bows and arrows."

The family philosophy was "*Más vale reutilizar que descartar,*" meaning, "Reusing is much more valuable than discarding." Examples of creative reuse also came from the adults in the community. Humberto remembers the beautiful, 25-pound cotton bags of "*La Piña*" flour in his home. Once those bags were empty, they became napkins, blouses and aprons.

The reuse examples extended to their food. In Juana's kitchen, nothing was wasted. She made tortillas at home. The tortillas they did not eat right away became tortilla chips (*totopos*). They used any leftover chips to make a tortilla chip and egg dish (*chilaquilles*). In Mexican households, pinto beans (*frijoles*) are a staple. They are first prepared by boiling them and serving them in a bowl and called *frijoles de la olla*. On the second day, they fry any leftover beans. Any beans that make it to the third day are refried.

As we have seen throughout this book, children growing up in poverty and forced to reuse household objects develop lifelong creativity. For Humberto, that early creativity and problem-solving led to his choice of study, and ultimately to his profession.

"Part of the reason I am an engineer is because I grew up always thinking about how to create things out of other things," Humberto acknowledges. "Later as a teenager, I tinkered with cars. I was driving cars by the time I was twelve. That is what older kids did in the country."

He had to earn the right to drive. From his older brothers, Humberto learned how to change the oil and wipers, and fix flat tires.

"The money we made working was our own money," Humberto says. "It wasn't considered household or family money. I bought my own gas and clothes, and even a car."

Humberto started working in the fields when he was nine years old. At fifteen, Humberto bought his first car for $900 cash—a red 1965 Ford Mustang—and immediately started modifying it. He was driving to high school in his own car before he ever took a driver's education course. "I also bought a 1939 Chevy Business Coupe for $125 during my sophomore year," he recalls. "It was all in pieces in a farmer's yard. We borrowed a trailer and gathered the pieces."

Many nights, after working at the local ice cream store, Humberto worked on this car under the lights of a "Welcome to El Centro Holiday Inn" sign lit up by high intensity discharge lights. "I turned two of those lights upside down and parked my '39 coupe under it. It was as bright as daylight," he recalls. "I remember the day I started that engine and took it out for a spin. My dad naturally thought I would later become a mechanic." However, Humberto knew he wanted to make things better, not just fix things.

The Job-Versus-College Decision

Humberto started school when he was three years old. He was allowed to attend primary school with his six-year-old sister. The rest of the Rincon children were working in the fields by this time.

"I learned to read before I started school," Humberto shares. "I taught my father how to read the names of the buses so he could ride the public bus system in Mexicali."

Later, his brother, who was studying accounting, forced Humberto to learn math early and challenged him with math quizzes.

"My brothers and cousins took me to the fields to help them," Humberto recalls. "They wanted me to learn how to work in the fields. What I learned was that I did not want to work there my entire life."

The family moved twice a year. He remembers that when he was nine years old, when the school year ended, he boarded a flatbed truck with wooden benches with his mother and his twelve-year-old sister. A man they called *Tio* Manuel drove for thirty hours up to

Washington State's Skagit Valley, directly north of Seattle. There, they worked with some Japanese strawberry growers for the summer.

"By then, my mom was 52 years old. Even with the two of us kids there, we didn't make much money that first summer," Humberto remembers. "In fact, we barely made enough to pay our fare back and buy some clothes for school. But by the next year, I was motivated. We worked faster and made more money."

Humberto enjoyed his summers in Washington State picking strawberries and cucumbers. He was happy to escape the unbearable heat of the Imperial Valley in southeastern California. He enjoyed the post-work socializing time. "Most kids called it 'labor camp.' To me it was 'summer camp.' I loved it!" he remembers. His mother promised he would never miss a day of school due to working in the fields. They always made it back to El Centro City before school started.

Humberto excelled in school, graduating high school with a "3.5-something GPA" in three and a half years, and in the top ten percent of his class. When he had finished all the courses needed for graduation, he went to work at the local Kinney Shoes® store. He was put directly into the management training program. Being bilingual in a town so close to the border meant good money in commissions. "My father thought I had made it—good money, good hours, lots of friends and a future with my own store promised to me."

His guidance counselor, Mr. Walker, was an African American man who spoke Spanish. "He coached me a lot and encouraged me to pursue math and science," Humberto reflects. "He told my parents 'your son could go to college.'" Humberto recalls his father's response, "Why would you want to go to college? You are already working at Kinney Shoes, making more money than me. You have great hours. Where will the money for college come from? You are going to give up this nice job where you wear a tie to go to college making no money for all those years?"

Humberto's guidance counselor was giving him advice that contradicted his father. "Mr. Walker told me there would be more money after college, much more than at the shoe store. I felt I had enough money already. But I really wanted to see if I could get into the automotive industry. Even though I had no role models who were engineers, I wanted the opportunity to try something different."

Humberto chose to apply for college and used his counselor's mailing address on his applications. He applied to UC Berkeley, UC Davis, UCLA, UC San Diego and Cal Tech at San Luis Obispo. Like many students in similar socioeconomic situations even today, he was focused only on taking the classes required for graduation. He didn't take pre-calculus or physics classes required for college admission and success. Those advanced classes were taken only by students who planned on going to college. However, Humberto was admitted to college under the Educational Opportunity Program. The EOP was designed to provide access to higher education to low-income and educationally disadvantaged students. This proved to be a definite academic disadvantage for a promising student who was encouraged to attend college so late in his senior year—and more so for Humberto who then decided to study engineering.

One day during his senior year of high school, Humberto returned from lunch to the shoe store. His boss, Mr. Griego, greeted him. "I've got some good news and some bad news. A big black man came in to tell you that you got admitted to college. The bad news is you're fired." Humberto explained, "Mr. Griego had been training me for management. He was introducing me to people and I was getting primed for my own store. I was the top accessories seller and I made great commissions." Once the boss recognized his own emotional reaction, he rehired Humberto as a part-time salesman. "I was off the management track," Humberto says with a smile.

Humberto joined his girlfriend's family on a road trip to visit different universities, because he, like her sister, had been accepted to a number of schools around California. They visited UC Berkeley, UC San Diego, UCLA, UC Davis and Cal Tech. Humberto's impressions of each campus have lasted through the decades.

"At UCLA, all I saw were cars and buildings. I definitely didn't want to go there. At UC Berkeley, there were kids everywhere smoking pot. The other two were nice, but I am not an ocean person. But at UC Davis, I felt at home. The open agricultural land and the smell of animals—I loved it. I chose this campus for my undergraduate studies because it was the only university not in a scary big city. It felt like the environment where I grew up—a farming town."

Now that Humberto had selected a college, he and his family prepared for the big move up north. Humberto wanted his father's support for his decision.

"Once my father understood a bit more about what engineers do, it allowed him to be supportive. He gave me a big amount of money, 4000 pesos (approximately $257 at the time), to go to college." For a farm laborer earning a low hourly wage, to save and give his son $257 to go to college was no small feat. That was a lot of money in 1974 and a huge gesture of support and love. Eleuterio surely felt a tremendous sense of pride. He was able to give his youngest son, and the only one to go to university, money for the next chapter in his life. Humberto applied for and received grants and scholarships to make up the difference.

Humberto remembers the trip north with his father. "He drove up to Davis with me in my 1939 coupe," Humberto reflects fondly. "We took a fourteen-hour road trip. That car did not go very fast. We had never done anything like that before—a father-son road trip."

On the road, Eleuterio reminisced about the different places he had worked as a *bracero*. He reflected on the different fields and types of produce he had worked with during his adult life. He then appreciated that his son would never know a life of hard labor. After Humberto showed his father the college campus, Eleuterio took a Greyground® bus home.

Educational Perseverance and Leadership
Humberto's choice of major came about like many other students. "When

I applied to college, I did not know the difference between engineering and architecture," he admits. "I knew both involved drawing and math which were two things I really enjoyed."

Humberto began taking all the required classes for first-year engineers at the same time: physics, calculus and math. Since he had not taken pre-calculus and physics classes in high school, this was Humberto's first exposure to these challenging subjects—and it was in college-level classes.

"I cried many nights, because I could not figure things out," Humberto reveals. "I would go to the teaching assistant, but he was a foreign student. I could not understand his English."

Humberto's friend Liz, who was a graduate student in teaching, consoled him and told him he needed to seek help. "In my physics class, there was a tall, handsome, brown-skinned guy with curly hair," describes Humberto. "He was over six feet in height. I wondered who he was and wondered if he was Mexican. His name was Ricardo." Humberto learned that Ricardo, a physics major who had served in the Navy, was doing fine in their physics class. "I asked Ricardo to help me with physics and he agreed. Later on, Ricardo confided that he helped me because he was afraid of me. He was assuming I was some sort of gang *cholo* who would beat him up!" This was Ricardo's viewpoint, despite Humberto's much smaller stature.

Humberto wondered if he was the only student struggling with these classes. "When I almost failed at the end of my first quarter, I started looking for brown faces I could ask for help. I found four others," Humberto remembers. "The five of us started a student self-help organization in 1975. We called it CALESS (Chicano and Latino Engineers and Scientists Society)." The five founders included Ricardo Urbanejo, the physics major, Humberto Rincon, the future mechanical engineer, Ernie, a civil engineer in the making, Richard, a geology major, and Narciso Gama, another mechanical engineer. CALESS represented students majoring in physics, engineering and geology.

"Ernie was from Bolivia and did not identify with the American term 'Chicano;' we threw in the 'Latino' for him. CALESS was an academic support and networking group. We reached out to others who were struggling with these classes. We visited their families. We helped them stay in school and persevere. We tutored pre-med students in their math and science classes. Some of my best friends were studying to become doctors."

The young Humberto, who struggled so much his first quarter, ultimately persevered through the toughest classes of his life. He specialized in mechanical engineering, and didn't stop there. Humberto eventually received a double bachelor of science degree in mechanical engineering and material science. And because Humberto never shies away from a challenge, he graduated with something else, something precious. Through CALESS, Humberto met a nutrition major named Geri. She and Humberto became parents during his junior year. Graduation day included his two degrees, a wife and his baby girl, Alejandrina.

After graduation, Humberto accepted a position with Pacific Bell Telephone on its management track program. Then, in a repeat of Humberto's earlier job-versus-college scenario, fate once again intervened to propel Humberto to even greater heights.

"We All Got Jobs."

Humberto credits three key influencers for his successful professional life: Mr. Walker, his high school guidance counselor, Ricardo, the Navy veteran turned physics major who helped him at UC Davis and finally, Dr. George Castro. While in school and working with CALESS, Humberto organized the first-ever Latino engineering and science symposium. It was 1976 and this event was early evidence of his keen ability to build his professional network. Dr. George Castro, a prominent scientist with a PhD from Cal Tech and the head of Physical Sciences at IBM® at the time, was the highest ranking Latino professional at that first symposium. The event attracted a huge turnout, complete with local TV coverage. Afterward, Dr. Castro invited the CALESS group to visit him at IBM.

"It became an annual event," Humberto explains. "We got lots of goodies, and it was a great trip."

During his senior year and on the verge of graduation, CALESS was on its annual field trip to IBM. Dr. Castro asked, "Are any of you guys going on to graduate school?"

"No, we all got jobs," Humberto responded.

Then Dr. Castro said, "That's too bad. I've got an unclaimed IBM full-ride scholarship for any school, specifically for a minority student who wants to pursue higher education in the sciences."

As Humberto told me this part of the story, my mind immediately went back to the Kinney Shoes story. I remembered the time Humberto was working in the shoe store, making money, wondering if his dad was right—wondering if leaving the job for a chance at education was the right thing to do. But this time, the young engineering student did not hesitate to bet on higher education.

Humberto recalls saying to Dr. Castro, "I'll take that scholarship."

"But first you've got to get accepted somewhere," Dr. Castro reminded him.

The application deadlines for the fall had already passed. Plus, Humberto says, "I was a father already. I had to convince my wife Geri that we could be poor students for one more year. I moved quickly and focused all my efforts and network to getting into Stanford."

The fruits of his efforts through CALESS paid off in a big way. John D. Kemper, the dean of the College of Engineering at UC Davis., was a friend and a supporter of CALESS. Humberto told him about the opportunity from Dr. Castro and IBM. The dean said, "You are a bit late in the process, but I will help you contact the admissions office at Stanford."

"I had also been appointed to an advisory council for the Regents of the University of California," Humberto explains. "I was advising the Chancellor on the specific needs of Latino students."

He contacted Professor Wilde at Stanford, a "pro-Latino" engineering professor at Stanford who had participated in the symposium. He mentioned the scholarship opportunity and his admissions timing problem. Putting his networking skills to use, remembering to tell the person he was asking for help what was in it for him, he mentioned that Stanford would get $20,000 from IBM as part of the graduate scholarship program.

Humberto's networking with Kemper, Wilde and the U.C. Regents was invaluable and opened doors for him. He was admitted to Stanford's graduate engineering program in an expedited manner. He was then awarded the full-ride scholarship from IBM, to pursue a master's degree in mechanical engineering design.

These extraordinary experiences shaped Humberto's professional foundation. He advises everyone, especially aspiring entrepreneurs, to "Be flexible. Be prepared to take advantage of opportunities that are presented to you. Be able to recognize the opportunity when it comes. The opportunity to go to the university was better than the shoe store. The opportunity to go to graduate school was better than the Pacific Bell Telephone opportunity. Opportunities are not obstacles. It's not that you're not committed to your original plan. Rather, you are exercising flexibility and taking the opportunity that has been put in front of you."

Then it was on to Stanford with Geri and little Alejandrina. His only regret: "I finished my master's degree in nine months. I wish I had slowed down and taken the two years. I wish I had been able to really absorb the Stanford environment—and gotten more sleep."

However Humberto says, "Being poor at Stanford was not a bad gig. My scholarship included a monthly stipend. We lived in married student housing with other couples, some of whom remain our friends to this day." He advises, "Don't rush through graduate school. I had to do it. My daughter was already two when I started school at Stanford."

- BS, Mechanical Engineering and Material Science, UC Davis
- MS, Mechanical Engineering Design, Stanford University
- Executive post-graduate training, Stanford University

Corporations and Startups

Since finishing his master's degree, Humberto has held senior positions at IBM and Seagate Technologies. Like many Silicon Valley engineers, he has also enjoyed assorted adventures with high-tech startups. He has worked to design, manufacture, improve and introduce complex technologies into various global markets. Along the way, he has taken additional executive-level courses to learn supply chain logistics and contract negotiations. He has also specialized in helping companies enter Asian markets and streamline their processes.

Where Humberto has applied his talents to innovate in the green economy comes from his childhood, using his resources efficiently to create better solutions. He is improving and reengineering our nation's inefficient industrial warehouse lighting.

I met with Humberto and electrical engineer Steve Montoya, Humberto's friend since the two met through CALESS at UC Davis. The men were working for a startup developing a better, smarter, industrial lighting fixture. Specifically, they were working to improve the high intensity discharge lighting (HID) found in America's largest interior spaces. Steve was the company's VP of Product Management and Engineering; Humberto the VP of Operations and Manufacturing.

"The work we are doing is focused on reducing the energy consumption and huge carbon footprint of America's warehouses," Steve explained.

The big box stores and their warehouses consume huge amounts of energy to light up immense spaces. Warehouses, distribution centers and retail spaces, create massive lighting needs and phenomenal energy consumption. Some estimate this lighting usage to be as high as 22 percent of annual U.S. energy consumption. [Source: www. lumetric.com/environmental_commitment]

The Primer on Industrial Lighting

How is warehouse HID lighting different from a standard incandescent light bulb? The light produced by an incandescent bulb is produced by a filament within a bulb. When the bulb is turned on, an electrical current goes through the filament; the current makes the element glow with heat which produces the light. The gas around the filament is there to slow down the decay of the filament and is not part of the source of light. HID lights are a bit more complex. These lights do not have a filament. Instead, the bulb contains electrodes that ignite a gas which produces the light. At ignition, a small amount of power creates an intense charge of electricity across the electrodes in the bulb. The charge excites the gas molecules, which discharge photon particles. This makes light based on glowing gas.

The basic idea of the product Steve and Humberto were developing was to incorporate computer-controlled digital technology to better manage and deliver the energy to these lamps. With this technology, the fixture can be managed as part of a network. Traditional HID bulbs are individual light sources that typically last 8000 hours. Newer bulbs can last up to 20,000 hours. HID lights will outlast traditional lights because HID lights are ignited and controlled under "gentler" conditions. There is a lot of room for improvement, a challenge engineers love to tackle. Steve and Humberto are dedicated to reducing the nation's large area lighting energy consumption.

The High Intensity Discharge lighting is divided into several sectors:
1. Big box/warehouse
2. Stadium
3. Street
4. Plant growing environments
5. Accent/external building

Their company chose big box stores and warehouses as their primary go-to-market entry point. "We chose California as the prime geographic target, given its unique position in terms of population density, energy cost and incentives to help offset the upgrade cost," Humberto explained.

"The world is waking up to the need for more efficiency in this type of lighting. Like changing our in-home bulbs to CFLs and LEDs, the need is being recognized to update commercial lighting. This technology is more than sixty years old. Not much has been done to make it more efficient. There's a lot of opportunity."

Here are the different approaches being used to revolutionize HID lighting:

1. **Reuse bulbs by controlling them at a central point to create smart lighting systems.** This makes existing HID bulbs controllable down to the individual light, and turns them into managed resources on a centralized network. Users can turn on essential lights only, where and when they are needed.

2. **Redefine what HID lighting looks like by improving its physics and chemistry.** This involves reengineering the bulb itself to get the gases to ignite differently. It is totally different technology, and also adds the ability to centrally control the bulbs.

3. **Apply LED technology from consumer accent lighting to industrial spotlighting.** Because LED light does not travel very far and diffuses quickly, the focus is on improving the reflector design and heat removal.

Company and Product

Humberto and Steve were working on engineering their lighting solution with a digital signal processor inside. This would enable two-way communication between a controller and the individual bulbs. This innovation would make it possible to tie an entire warehouse full of HID lights to a wireless network infrastructure and the building's control systems. Additionally, each light would be able to provide feedback on its status. They were creating the opposite of today's analog, standalone light bulb.

"The play was to bring this technology up-to-date," Humberto explained. "It is possible to manage and optimize the ignition and energy usage to create a more efficient system. Through software and external monitoring of the ambient light, we were also able to make the lighting smarter, and reduce energy usage further by having only the amount of light needed on at any time."

If a huge regional distribution center can control interior lighting down to the single unit bulb, it can have all lights off except for one particular row where loading/unloading is taking place. These new, smart, super-efficient light bulbs can cut the energy usage of warehouses significantly. They could slash the amount of energy they consume, and reduce their utility bills significantly.

"My personal motivation to go for the savings was natural given my upbringing. I do my absolute best in everything to minimize waste," says Humberto. "Out of the box, that solution can slash 25 percent of the electricity needed over current HID lighting technology. As you control the lighting network, light can be provided on demand exactly where you need it. The energy savings can exceed sixty percent."

Humberto is applying the family philosophy about reuse from his childhood *"Más vale reutilizar que descartar"* to this innovation. He explains, "We've designed this product to accept current reflector technology—the large dome typically made of plastic, aluminum or glass—in use by our customers. This means we don't have to replace the reflectors—they can be re-used. This further reduces the amount of waste and footprint associated with updating warehouse lighting." Why not apply the concept of reuse to reinventing lighting on a large scale?

"This is the sector I feel passionate about. I believe that every erg (a unit of energy and mechanical work) you never need is the best green thing you can do. I am constantly asking myself, 'what can we do to save energy?' The way I see it, you can find ways to produce more energy or find ways to not need as much of it. It is important that we research and innovate on both sides of this. I chose the latter."

Humberto is also waste-conscious in his personal life. He telecommutes, prints documents only when necessary, manages his water usage and has replaced his home lighting with CFL where appropriate. He recycles and reuses everything, including lumber. He has grown a produce garden at home since childhood.

Humberto observes, "There are more visible options today at the consumer level, increasing my level of participation in conservation efforts. CFL is one example. However, what is needed is a new paradigm. Consumers often find that to 'go green' involves having to spend more money. Green products are not necessarily cheaper. I have done my own comparisons. I've looked at new products versus those made from recycled products. The recycled product is often more expensive and that bothers me. Part of it is explained by the cost of pre- and post-processing that needs to be done, but I believe that some companies are taking advantage of the green movement too."

At press time, Humberto was evaluating two potential career moves to continue working on reducing energy consumption. One was to join a Fortune 500 company. The other was to join his lifelong friend, Steve, at another startup to improve the chemistry within the bulb chamber. This is totally different technology and no doubt will surely create an entirely new industry. Whichever path he chooses next, Humberto is committed to making these needed improvements.

Final Thoughts from the Engineer
Humberto says his pride and joy is the CALESS organization, which just celebrated its 35th anniversary and boasts over 300 alumni. At the anniversary celebration, Humberto was asked to deliver the keynote speech having presented at the organization's *quinceañera*—15th anniversary and the 25th anniversary. The fact that CALESS is still going strong is a mixed blessing. Its continued need raises questions about the preparedness levels of kids like Humberto who are entering college in the 21st century. "New students are still experiencing the same problems we experienced back then," he states. "Why are they still struggling?"

Perhaps, like Humberto, many Latino kids don't believe they are college material because adults in their lives do not tell them they are. In some communities, parents say things like, "People like us do not go to college" or even "You can't go to college because we have no money." As a result, they focus on taking the minimum classes needed to graduate high school so they can start working. This creates an academic challenge especially if they later decide to go to college. This may be why students continue to need CALESS today. Humberto and Steve recently donated seed money to CALESS to start an advisory council, and they want CALESS to get an official physical space on campus.

Talking with Humberto in his garden, I observed his joy as he reflected on what is happening with the green movement today. "Today's environmental movement is a commercial one," he feels. "Things that are true conservation are not really new. It's what I have done my whole life. I have this small garden at my home. I reuse lumber. Today people see you reusing things and label you a miser. But I just will not throw things away that can serve another purpose. I remain hopeful for a change in more people's attitudes toward reuse and conservation."

Humberto Recommends

"I monitor two sites that interest me for their focus on entrepreneurship in the energy reduction and alternative energy technologies."

• FountainBlue's Clean Energy Entrepreneurs' Forum at www.fountainblue.biz

• Bio Fuel Digest at www.biofuelsdigest.com

The Rocky Mountain Institute is another source for energy-centric technology and can be found at www.rmi.org.

For high school students who wish to study engineering and work to reduce energy usage, Humberto offers these words of wisdom:
"You are in the best position to change the world. You can help form it so you can have a clean environment with sufficient resources to live comfortably. There are many contributions and areas where you can

help today before you start a technical degree. Remember first: don't waste, don't contaminate and do leave your surroundings better than you found them. Each and every one of us can do that within our immediate environments. With our collective efforts, we will have significant global impact.

"I joined our town's 'Carbon Diet Club' which focuses on waste reduction and minimizing the carbon footprint. Look to see if your town has one and encourage your family and neighborhood to participate. Your local energy company may also have information on their website on how to save energy, and how to take advantage of their resources to help you identify areas where you can save.

"From a career selection perspective, pursue your passion as you dis-cover it. Always try to apply it in an environmentally-responsible way."

For college students, Humberto offers this advice:

"College is where you build your career foundation, define your principles and identify your values. This is where you start building your network. These principles, values and networks are what will propel and support you as you fill your tool box with the variety of skills you will need to succeed. This tool box has both hard and soft skills—your technical and people skills. The students you are with today are all developing and building themselves too. Soon you'll disperse to various corners of the world. Your lives will intersect in the future. Their level of success will vary and the influence they have will vary, but you will always have that bonding from your college days. Don't ever lose it. Stay connected to your peers and your alma mater. Join your respective professional organization and your alumni association. Help others around you in whatever way you can, be it with time, money or advice. It will all pay dividends for you in the future. Use all of the resources around you and keep up with technology once you leave college. Never stop learning, nor exploring. Be ready to recognize opportunities. Be able to change your path or make different decisions if it will get you to your higher end goal. Today's careers are very dynamic; you must have a portable toolbox. Be ready to take that toolbox and your network wherever you go."

For professionals in a mid-career transition, Humberto offers this:

"My advice to practicing engineers is to take your current skill set and look at ways to apply it to revolutionize clean tech, or apply existing technologies to develop new solutions. There are many opportunities to create energy with renewable resources and ways to apply this to transportation, at home or in industry. My own favorite applications are ones that reduce consumption of our natural resources, and decrease pollution and the consequences of our waste on our fragile planet. We must all work together to decrease our carbon footprint.

"One area that we should all be concerned about is a source of clean potable water—for us and for future generations. Everything needs water to thrive and we are using a lot of it. We are contaminating water with our lifestyle and not conserving enough.

There are many opportunities to make an impact. Take your passion and apply it in ways that could help. Opportunities in the above areas can be found in many places. The obvious ones are among the many startups working in these fields now. Some established Fortune 500 companies are doing it. You can learn more through your formal LinkedIn® network or your informal network. Your professional society is always a very good source of opportunities as are the publications your alumni association provides. Again, I encourage you to stay connected. I connected with that first startup company through Steve Montoya, a classmate from UC Davis who I met through CALESS 35 years ago. Yes, there are formal channels specific to the various sectors you may be interested in pursuing. But more importantly, the network comes from everyone around you. You can never know what will present itself, or from which connection."

Photo by Brent Bear

Humberto in his garden at home
www.linkedin.com/pub/humberto-rincon/3/649/7b5

Monica DeZulueta, PhD
Greening the World with Software

$\mathcal{D}$r. Monica DeZulueta's engineering work is directly responsible for taking many cars off the road. She has made it possible for people to commute less frequently and to avoid or reduce their air travel for business purposes. Monica is an innovator at Microsoft® Corp. She is a principal data platform technology specialist, which is fancy language for a communications systems guru.

Monica does not own her own business, yet she is an innovative force for new, greener solutions to vexing environmental problems. She is a great example of being an innovator as an employee of a large enterprise. The key is to work in an industry whose products and services enable positive environmental and economic impacts. In Monica's case it's the unified communications and collaboration industry.

I worked in this industry after completing my master's degree in international management. It is transforming how people work locally, nationally and globally. It is redefining the meaning of productivity in global business. It is changing *how much* we travel and *if* we travel. The technologies created by the companies in this industry are among the most influential green economy enablers. There will be many career opportunities in this industry for decades to come.

As a child, Monica's parents, Concepción and Luis Alberto, told her, "There are only two things that nobody can ever take away from you—what is in your heart and what is in your head."

They knew this personally because they had left Cuba with nothing except what was in their hearts and heads. They came to the United States for a life of freedom. Monica's grandmother Isabel later arrived in Miami just five days before baby Monica entered the world. Monica and her younger brother were raised with a strong service ethic and a green lifestyle. Her parents taught her that nothing goes to waste. They intentionally bought foods that served multiple purposes.

"We reused a lot of food," Monica recalls. "The bone of the animal got used to flavor a stew, as did leftover potatoes and ham. I was taught to eat well and cheaply. I ate a lot of lentils. No food ever went to waste—it made us think creatively." Her parents bought a house with eight mango trees. "We made mango ice cream and other mango desserts. We gave away mangos, but we never wasted a mango."

Grandmother Isabel had many *dichos* (sayings), all with a message. They inspired Monica to create her own sayings. "*Deja al futuro mejor que el pasado y el presente*"—Leave the future better than the past and the present. This was truly a forward-looking mindset for a young person.

Monica remembers being influenced by the public service announcements that aired in the 1970s. "There was a commercial with a Native American Indian crying. He was looking at the wasteland that America had become. It is a particularly vivid memory for me. I also remember the 'Give a hoot, don't pollute' campaign that starred an owl." She laments that today's public service announcements are lacking this key message about preservation.

Monica's Aunt Eugenia was also influential and personified the values Monica was taught. Monica remembers her aunt working full-time while studying for her graduate degree, all the while generously donating to the poorest churches in Miami. During the holiday season, her family sponsored a family in need.

Monica attended an all-girls school called Carrollton School of Sacred Heart in Miami, founded in the 1800s by a Catholic nun. This progressive nun believed that if you educate girls, you educate a society. The nun believed this because her brother, a Jesuit priest, had educated her.

"Every girl in my family has attended a Sacred Heart school," Monica shares. "My female ancestors attended Sacred Heart Schools in Paris, Boston, Havana and Miami. Grandma Isabel attended Sacred Heart in Havana. My mom was in the last graduating class at Sacred Heart in Cuba before government commandos took over the school, stole it from the nuns and turned it into a state-run medical school."

Monica was the fifth generation to be educated through this school. Her daughter was the sixth.

"The mission of the school defined me from the seventh grade through my senior year of high school."

That mission is:
    1. A personal and active faith in God
    2. A deep respect for intellectual values
    3. A social awareness that impels to action
    4. The building of community as a Christian value
    5. Personal growth in an atmosphere of wise freedom
[Source: Carrollton School of Sacred Heart]

Based on this mission, Monica's school focused her on community service. "I was required to do charity work. We each picked our own charity and volunteered. The message was: 'You have been fortunate to have a good life. Now you must give back to others.'"

Monica excelled in math and science. "I had a fantastic biology and chemistry teacher named Mr. Crockwell," Monica tells. "He brought robotics to Carrollton. My favorite classes were analytical. I enjoyed Shakespeare too, but for entertainment only. I wanted to apply math and science knowledge—that meant studying engineering."

Florida International University selected two students from each high school to attend free summer classes. Monica was chosen and took a computer engineering course. She fell in love with computers.

"That is when I changed my mind from studying chemical engineering to electrical engineering," Monica explains. "I realized I was interested in the applications, not just the pure programming."

With high school in her rear-view mirror and a pocketful of Advanced Placement credits, Monica enrolled as an engineering student at Florida International University in 1983. During her freshman year, along with handling a full academic load, she completed her open water SCUBA certification. A lifetime of snorkeling and diving in a nearby reef in the Florida Keys helped her gauge how we are doing in protecting our environment. It also influenced her later career choices around disseminating technology that improves sustainable practices on a large scale.

Her engineering summer internships included working at the National Oceanic and Atmospheric Administration, on its hurricane reconnaissance airplane, the P-3 Orion. After graduating in 1986 at the age of twenty, Monica worked for NASA. Her first job was at the shuttle launch and payload processing center.

"When you hear 'go for launch' on TV during a launch, they are using a giant communications system with hundreds of channels. I was part of building that system," she says.

Monica's work at NASA exposed her to Microsoft's technologies where she learned about and created embedded systems. After a few years, her managers saw Monica's leadership potential, and nominated her for an on-campus engineering management degree program. Professors from the University of Central Florida conveniently came to the NASA base to teach its future leaders. Monica's two children were born during these early NASA years.

I asked why she was not still working for NASA, a place where an engineer could spend an entire career. "I became an engineer to be innovative, not to do the same thing forever. Monica says of her time at NASA, "I left NASA when my system was going operational. That same system is still in use today."

When Monica's husband received a job transfer, the family moved back to Miami. "My husband had followed me up there to work for NASA. It was my turn to follow him back. We wanted our kids to have a solid education and the opportunity to attend great schools," Monica explained. Fortunately, the UCF engineering management classes she started while at NASA were recorded, allowing her to finish her master's degree through the Florida Engineering Education Delivery System (FEEDS).

She then landed a position with Coulter Corporation's research department working for a well-respected innovator, the inventor of the CBC (Complete Blood Count) machine. There, she built on her skills from NASA, adding valuable experiences to her expanding engineering tool kit.

"We would develop new applications for other industries using existing technologies," she said. "It was an environment of constant innovation."

Monica thrived there. Unfortunately, when the founder died, the company was sold and split apart. Moving on, she applied to Microsoft Consulting Services (MCS) and landed a position in Miami. At MCS she worked with different industries and was directly involved in the implementation and deployment phases of major projects.

For three years, Monica programmed databases and other systems to work together. This helped employees within these organizations work more productively, using information more efficiently, ultimately laying the foundation for the work she does today.

- BS, Electrical Engineering from Florida International University
- MSEE, Computer Engineering
- Master's in Engineering Management from the University of Central Florida
- PhD, Electrical Engineering (FIU)

The Primer on the Unified Communications and Collaboration Industry

This industry merges business telecommunications and the Internet. The Internet and its data networks have enabled communications modes like email, instant messaging, video and audio conferencing to become widespread and common. Most people working in corporate settings prefer to collaborate via voice even though they also use other communications technologies. This is important when teams never meet in person, yet work on the same project. They need to meet regularly, and they have strict timelines. The voice communication they use may be over traditional landline telephones or mobile phones on cellular networks. It may use voice over the Internet protocol (VoIP—think Skype®) on laptops, or go through specialized multi-band phones that can receive and transmit voice signals over both cellular and VoIP networks. They also use mobile video conferencing like with the iPhone®. In addition, these teams must access information that traditionally was only accessible if they were on-site.

The problem is that each of these modes of communication was developed as a separate system and not technically capable of communicating with dissimilar systems. For example, your company's secure instant messaging system was not meant to run on your mobile device, and your corporate video conferencing system was likely not developed to be taken off-site. Plus, many corporate databases were designed to be accessed only from a physical office. To function, employees had to drive to the office to do their work because of technological limitations and restrictions.Many risk-averse organizations still operate this way, which forces employees to commute and travel extensively.

The industry has used three terms—*unified communications, collaboration* or *unified collaboration*—interchangeably in the context of enterprise communications. They refer to a technology platform capable of providing the user with multiple communication modes, all designed to work together. Think secure communications dashboard, with all the great toys available to you on whatever device you use. For example, you may start a three-way instant messaging chat with two colleagues, but then with a few clicks on the dashboard, turn the IM chat into a video conference to share new sketches or prototypes.

With an advanced collaboration system like this, the very idea of work begins to change. You no longer have to drive to work. You and your team can function as if you were physically together, even though everyone is scattered all over the globe. Work becomes *what you do* instead of *where you are*. Organizations using these systems enable employees to work from wherever they need to be, including a home office. This means that telecommuting stops being a perk for the few and becomes a widespread corporate social and environmental initiative. Creating a corporate culture that requires its employees to commute less is a much greener alternative. This anti-commuting option results in operational savings from less real estate needed, less energy used, fewer desks, fewer phones, less of everything. Telecommuting greatly improves a company's green credentials. Investing in sophisticated collaboration systems takes cars off the road and gets people out of airports and airplanes. This greener, more flexible corporate culture becomes an excellent employee retention tool and a recruiting highlight to attract new, eco-minded employees.

A few examples from elsewhere in the industry will help you appreciate the positive environmental impact unified communications systems are creating today. Colombian-born Andres Maz works for Cisco Systems® as Head of Policy for Latin America. Here's how he uses his company's collaboration systems to work globally and in an eco-friendly way.

- "I telecommute at least twice a week using our technology. My corporate IP phone makes it possible for people to call my office number and reach me wherever I am. By not commuting, I'm reducing emissions, plus I get two hours of extra time each day to spend with my daughter."

- "I use TelePresence (Cisco's high-definition video conferencing system) to meet with people in Latin America. I can attend meetings with high-level policy officials and private sector leaders in the region. We meet face-to-face via video as if we are in the same place. After fifteen minutes we forget we are not."

• "We can do both one-to-one video calls and multi-point connections for larger conferences. My internal Global Policy team used to meet twice a year with members in India, Singapore, England, California, Washington D.C. and Belgium. In just this one team example, we saved twenty people from traveling twice. That's forty international and domestic trips not taken. That is real money and real carbon emissions that we avoided."

• "Most of my colleagues from the Latin American region are home-based. They are working in huge cities of millions of people. They do not want to commute. We have a corporate policy of maintaining mobile offices, shared offices (known as 'hoteling') and reducing our consumption of real estate on a global basis. This means we consume less energy for air conditioning, lighting and everything else while keeping our people productive."

Cisco Systems announced savings of over $400 million through travel avoidance in a twelve-month period. Clearly, corporations utilizing collaboration systems like these are saving real money while doing their part to green the environments where they operate. What is exciting is that most businesses will eventually be using at least some of these innovations. This is because they provide both environmental and operational (economic) savings. The types of careers being created as more corporations adopt collaboration technologies include:

• Technical sales engineers (the engineer on the sales team)

• Sales account managers and sales reps trained in solution-selling techniques (versus selling a product)

• Professional services consultants (to understand the business processes that need to be improved and to match the appropriate technologies to the new solution)

- Engineers to do the network analysis, system design, project implementation, testing and programming customized capabilities

- Project managers who oversee the project's timeline, budget and people resources and are responsible for keeping projects on schedule

- Marketers who can understand the technologies, creating effective messaging to communicate the benefits, present to potential clients, and write case studies of successful implementations

- Product managers to lead the teams that bring new versions of innovative products to market

In the relatively young unified communications (UC) and collaboration industry that is merging different technologies using a wide variety of approaches, there are many companies grouped into three basic vendor types. Those with:

- a telecommunications heritage, such as Avaya®, Siemens® Enterprise Communications, Alcatel-Lucent®

- a hardware heritage, such as Cisco Systems, IBM, NEC®, Toshiba®

- a software heritage, such as SAP®, Microsoft, Interactive Intelligence®. This includes many small companies that are creating new, web-based platforms from scratch, with an eye toward avoiding the trickier technical problems of integrating older systems.

Monica works for a company in the latter group, Microsoft Corporation, considered by many to be the established leader in the UC space.

Dr. DeZulueta's Role in the Innovation
In 2006, Monica left MCS because the company wanted her to travel frequently. Instead, she switched into a pre-sales engineer role called a TSP (Technical Systems Professional). She began to service the big companies on the east coast, working for Microsoft's Technology Centers. In this role, she established some goodwill with the Microsoft Federal team by doing successful proofs of concept

and attending architectural design sessions requiring her expertise. When a position opened up on that team, they wanted her to join them. They did not care where she lived.

Monica is now a principal data platform architect and works within the Public Sector Division. Microsoft's Federal Team, largely based in Washington D.C., is dedicated to serving and greening our largest military and civilian agencies, plus large defense contractors. They serve the Department of Energy and the Veterans Administration. These agencies are implementing large-scale green initiatives and deploying Microsoft systems, making commute avoidance possible for their employees. Monica's work helps them dramatically reduce carbon footprints by taking employees out of cars and airplanes, yet still conducting business effectively.

Monica shared that the U.S. Treasury Department is specifically interested in reducing its energy usage, costs and overall carbon footprint. They want to "virtualize" their systems, meaning to reduce the amount of hardware used. Downsizing hardware systems reduces power requirements. Another approach modernizes in-place systems with newer servers. Many government agencies and large corporations have very old energy-hogging computer hardware. Newer servers are energy-efficient and can run far more advanced software applications. They can also run more applications per server, resulting in less hardware. Monica has a hands-on role engineering the specific solutions to make this happen. She must create a new design for each system for each agency. Each existing technology environment is unique. Each new project requires a team that collaborates to create a unique solution. At Microsoft, these teams, called Specialized Technical units (STU), are composed of systems engineers who meet with government customers.

"We start with a strategy briefing with the customer. We discuss and present our standard options and architectures," Monica explains. "We meet and do an architectural design session. Then we tailor our technologies to their needs. This may lead to a proof of concept, to bringing in our professional services group or to engaging a partner to do a custom deployment based on our design."

In a few years, when the Treasury Department becomes a model of energy efficiency, Monica will know that she was directly involved in making this happen.

On the contractor side, Monica notes that Lockheed Martin® has many engineers who telecommute. "They only go into their offices once a week."

Her team has enabled thousand of engineers to work seamlessly from home offices and avoid commuting four days a week. What is more environmentally-friendly than avoiding a commute? Her team also makes it possible for employees to gain secure access to information held in their corporate databases from wherever they're working.

The smartest companies use their own technologies. In this industry, your employer typically expects you to use these technologies and encourages you to work remotely at least a few days a week. It helps the sales teams answer questions from potential customers like, "How many of your employees work from home at least half time?" or "How secure is this access for your home-based workers?" If a company creating these collaboration products and services is not using them, it is extremely difficult to sell them.

Deploying these tools to its global workforce saves Microsoft piles of money. Employees can collaborate with customers in real time and face-to-face, while not spending money on hotels, taxis and airfare. This reduces the global corporation's carbon footprint and improves its green credentials versus its competitors. Plus, in deploying collaboration technologies to its own workforce, Microsoft has employees evangelizing the value of their solutions. This value can be found both in how the solutions help to green their environments, and with the long list of daily lifestyle benefits.

The Motivation to Work in This Industry
Monica works from her Miami home fifty percent of the time. She is fully equipped with Microsoft technologies like Office® Communicator System for instant and unified messaging, Windows® 7 with power consumption monitoring, Live Meeting® for web-based

collaboration, and Round Table®, a video conferencing system with a 360-degree view. These systems enable her to collaborate frequently with her Washington D.C.-based team. She can conduct product demonstrations and communicate with customers while avoiding spewing carbon emissions.

She shares, "Our U.S. government customers know it is impractical for me to get on a plane from Florida to D.C. just to have a one-hour meeting. They understand the need to do meetings remotely using available collaboration technologies."

These technologies have afforded her the opportunity to be near her growing children while serving customers. Many professionals envy this desirable lifestyle improvement. Monica's green lifestyle includes walking to the grocery store with her own personal shopping cart. She started this walk when gas topped four dollars a gallon and decided to continue it, even when gas prices dropped down a bit. She has discovered that walking also results in high quality family time. She and her husband decided they could share a car for the little driving they do, becoming a one car family. In her home, she has ditched her halogen bulbs for CFL bulbs, and replaced an old air-conditioning unit with a newer, highly efficient one. Monica also monitors her home energy usage by leveraging the Microsoft Hohm® site.

Clearly, someone with Monica's talent, education and experience could write her own ticket to anywhere. Professionally, she knows she has many options, yet she has stayed with Microsoft for ten years. She explains, "The reason for staying at Microsoft is the chance to work for a company that is interested in making a difference and being innovative. By designing systems for the government, I know I am making an impact on a grand scale."

For an engineer like Monica, who is all about the innovation process, this role is important in another way. Take notice, because it is highly instructive for those seeking a career that will continuously evolve. "I am also involved with the database product teams," she shares. "I serve as a liaison between our public sector customers and our product teams. I tell the product team how customers use our products and what their needs are. I've been involved in product planning for solutions that are three to four years away."

Monica has a direct impact on Microsoft's *future* innovations. Plus, Monica says that when she started working for Microsoft, Bill Gates told all the new hires during the United Way® kick-off campaign, "We will take good care of you. We expect you to take care of others."

For Monica, who has been doing community service work since she was fifteen years old at Sacred Heart school, this corporate commitment to social responsibility is a big deal. "Microsoft gives corporate matches of up to $12,000 per employee per year. They expect us to use this benefit," she explains.

Monica is heavily involved in Microsoft's DigiGirlz, a mentoring group that targets and inspires minority girls to pursue careers in technology. She has been an active mentor for over a decade and speaks at schools in D.C. and Florida. She donates time and money to organizations addressing the under-representation of minorities in technology fields, and she is focused on developing more innovators into the future.

"I have mentored kids who are now in their own careers and mentoring other kids," she shares. "I am like the grandmother mentor. I have a picture of me with the young lady I mentored and the girl she is mentoring now—three generations of mentoring in one picture."

She also gives back to her Sacred Heart school, where it all began. "I have developed a curriculum I use to teach kids about robotics. It is basic programming in a simple and fun way." She mentors students enrolled in the biology and chemistry classes taught by her high school teacher Mr. Crockwell.

Monica is also committed to Microsoft because of the corporation's deep commitment to sustainable business practices and encouraging employees to participate. "At our Redmond headquarters campus, we have transit connector shuttles, a fleet of Prius® cars, other hybrid vehicles and employee shuttles," she explains. "Our cafeteria utensils and plates are all biodegradable plastic. We reuse PCs throughout the employee population so that everyone has exactly the computing power they need."

Microsoft employees like Monica have real power to dramatically reduce personal and corporate emissions on a global level. They are doing it today as the corporation adds more jobs around the globe and spreads the deployment of green collaboration technologies to the world's government agencies, global enterprises and smaller companies. Because she and Microsoft are creating and deploying these solutions every day, fewer people are commuting in their cars to work each day. The net overall reduction in greenhouse gases as a result of commute-avoidance that is made possible by Microsoft's technologies is unknown. However, if the examples here are any indication, the overall trend is excellent. There are more engineering and support jobs being created to deploy unified communications and collaboration technologies, and that will improve the quality of the environment in many communities.

As you look at your career options, ask about the company's environmental and sustainability initiatives. Communicate that these things matter to you and that you're evaluating potential employers based on these criteria. It's true that talent follows money—it always has. Whether or not you choose the employer that offers you the highest salary, an employer's lifestyle programs may affect your choice too. Increasingly, professional talent is following the real green credentials and commute-avoidance initiatives of America's companies.

Recently Monica and her children were on a glass-bottom boat at that special reef she's enjoyed her entire life. The reef is part of the John Pennekamp National Marine Reserve in the Florida Keys. Fortunately, this piece of the world is exactly as she remembers it since childhood. She is happy her children are enjoying it now in the same pristine condition. This keeps her motivated to adopt as many sustainable practices as possible in her personal and professional life, and to help others do the same. She hopes this reef can be exactly as it is today when her future grandchildren take up snorkeling.

Monica's daughter and son are both attending engineering school in Massachusetts at Worcester Polytechnic Institute. They are following in their mother's footsteps to see how they can apply their talents to change the world for the better.

Monica Recommends

Monica's advice for anyone interested in working in the collaboration software industry is, "At the core, collaboration solutions are all about teamwork. This is something that everyone interested in collaboration needs to demonstrate."

Specifically, for high school students who want to apply their talents in the unified communications and collaboration industry she offers, "Load up on math and science classes. If your high school is lacking in math and science classes, do not let that stop you. Take some at your local community college. Prepare yourself to study engineering. It provides a solid basis for technical and critical thinking. It also provides the opportunity to excel at lab work, which emphasizes team work."

She recommends the following organizations for students:

- IEEE Women in Engineering—www.ieee.org/membership_services/membership/women/index.html

- Society of Hispanic Professional Engineers (SHPE)—www.oneshpe.shpe.org

- Junior Engineering Technical Society (JETS)—www.jets.org

- Society of Women Engineering (SWE)—www.societyofwomen engineers.swe.org

"Participation in groups like these offers great benefits to you. They often provide you with guidance on technology as well as the opportunity to engage with peers and experienced professionals. You can find mentors there, and they often offer scholarships to students active in their organizations."

If you are already in college and are interested in working in this industry, she advises this:

"Study engineering. It provides a solid basis for technical and critical thinking as well as lots of lab work, which emphasizes team work. Get involved in organizations you are passionate about. People who merge their passion with their studies or career are happier and more productive. Such involvement shows commitment as well as the ability to work well in teams. There are many events you can attend as you begin networking. These include IEEE and other professional functions, the local computer user groups, environmental group functions and university guest lectures. If you wish to engage with professionals, just check out the business section of the local newspaper. You will find different business networking events often available at reduced rates to students.

Regardless of your career choice, the ability to work well with others is a key factor to a successful career. Working on your communications skills is also important. You can be passionate and have innovative ideas, but if you cannot communicate these great ideas and thoughts to others, then it is all for naught. Improving your communications skills is also imperative as you build your portfolio of skill sets.

Attend IEEE dinners, which are open to members and guests, including students. Your local universities hold lectures and invite speakers from all over the world on a variety of topics. These are posted on their websites and are open to everyone interested in the specific topic. In South Florida, there are several computer users groups where companies like Microsoft will do presentations on their new technologies. For environmentally-focused groups, the Fairchild Gardens provides opportunities to all age ranges to learn about the Florida ecology. The rangers at the National and State Parks also provide a wealth of knowledge for those interested in their ecological surroundings."

For professionals in a mid-career transition who wish to enter this industry, Monica offers this:

"I would recommend a graduate degree in engineering if possible. If not possible, then get an MBA with an MIS focus. This will give you a technical focus and the ability to work in teams. Remember that collaboration at its core is about teamwork. If a graduate degree seems impossible, a graduate certificate may be another route. Some certificate programs are only a few months, or even a few weeks, long. If you are considering a transition or wish to enter this industry, attend events hosted by organizations such as IEEE, SHPE and NSHMBA (National Society of Hispanic MBAs)."

Please see the Additional Resources section in the back of the book for more about this industry. The trend-watching resources included there are among the best I used when working in that industry.

Monica delivering a web conference and customer demo from her home office/
engineering lab
www.linkedin.com/pub/monica-dezulueta/4/693/943

Robert Zardeneta
Saving Lives, Creating Leaders with Green Building Techniques

*S*tart with kids in East Los Angeles pushed out of traditional education. Add innovative thinkers versed in green building techniques eager to fix up dilapidated homes for low-income families. The result was a unique non-profit organization featured in the Obama administration's "United We Serve" campaign—LA CAUSA, an acronym for "Los Angeles Communities Advocating for Unity, Social Justice and Action."

Robert Zardeneta, Executive Director of LA CAUSA, says, "We work with the young people left behind by the 'No Child Left Behind' Act. We are a non-profit youth leadership organization with a mission to empower young people to become agents of change within their community."

What if you could rid your community of blight by turning unsafe homes into models of green housing? What if you could improve the health of a neighborhood's population? What if you could rescue and remediate high school dropouts and gang members through green building skills and leadership programs? What if you could create green jobs for these skilled employees year after year and keep them working toward community improvement? What if the kids you rescued became college graduates and policymakers and perpetuated this cycle? And what if you could do all this good from within one single non-profit organization?

Some people seek leadership positions they are qualified to fill, hoping for a good match. For Robert however, leadership opportunities in community service seem to find him. The result is life-changing, job-creating, environmentally rooted social justice-based community building at its absolute best. Let's learn how it's happening in East L.A.

Growing Up in East L.A.

Robert Zardeneta was born in East L.A. to Robert and Graciela Zardeneta. Robert's parents took pride in their East L.A. roots and in being hippies. Robert Senior was a Vietnam Veteran who had served as a military training instructor. After leaving the service, he worked for the City of Los Angeles for thirty years.

"My father showed me the importance of being committed to public service," Robert recalls. "He taught me to be proud of where we came from. He did community development work in the city, helping homeowners improve their homes. He took me to work with him and showed me the results. He had the biggest impact in my life."

Robert had a strong sense that his father's energy and efforts made tangible differences in peoples' lives in his community. His father loved sports and coaching kids. He loved acting like a kid when playing games. Robert suspects this was because his father didn't have much of a childhood—he had been the middle child in a single-parent household with eleven children.

Robert Junior developed a deep love of music and aspired to be a musician. He learned the rich history of the music and art of East L.A. Robert says he was a sharp student, not a good student, at Garfield High School. He did the work, yet didn't find it challenging. He eventually enrolled in the high school's computer science magnet program. He took Advanced Placement (AP) courses to prepare for higher education. There he got his first glimpse of leadership.

"I was interested in leadership, but not in planning proms," he reflects. "Instead, I was on the shared decision-making council where we handled school improvements. It included community members and student representatives. I fought with teachers to get stuff like lockers."

Keep that scene in mind—taking on teachers to improve things for the students—as you read the rest of his story.

The Student Figuring Out the Path

Pursuing his dream to become a musician, Robert was accepted into the Berkelee College of Music in Boston, with a jazz/voice scholarship. The school was 3,000 miles and a world away from the culture and environment of Robert's childhood. "I moved to Boston in July. I actually wore a sweater on the airplane," Robert shares. "I was fully expecting to see snow when I got there. I was very homesick and had identity issues. People would ask me 'What are you?' because they had never met anyone of Mexican descent. I felt the racial tension and was very uncomfortable. Plus, there were no taco trucks in Boston. I partied too much, got laryngitis and eventually came home."

Robert's dream to become a musician didn't come true, which turned out to be lucky for many kids today. He took some time to regroup, tried out different schools and reflected on his life. He realized that, outside of his father, he didn't have good role models. The ones he had at the time encouraged the rock star in him, but never told him he was a smart kid.

Robert became a teaching assistant at El Sereno Middle School in northeast L.A at the age of eighteen. Robert says, "The little heavy metal kids gravitated to me. I started playing my guitar with them after school and kept them out of trouble. I saw myself in these kids and became the role model I never had." He made the conscious choice to not encourage them to be rock stars. He urged them to stay in school and be successful. Robert played music after hours and did well with it until one day the worst drawbacks of the lifestyle became apparent. "In 1996, a very talented musician friend of mine died by jumping off a bridge," he shares. "I quit playing music right after that."

However, Robert had discovered that working with young students was very fulfilling. Around that time, Walt Hazzard, UCLA's renowned men's basketball coach, founded the L.A. Sports Academy, an after-school pilot program targeting the development of student athletes at the middle school level. It was a partnership between L.A. Unified School District and UCLA. Richard Alatorre, a councilman who knew of Robert through the middle school, recruited him. Robert became a successful basketball coach at the sports academy. "I was successful, because I taught life skills as a coach," he states. "Our students graduated with an average GPA of 3.0 at this school. I counseled them to focus on school first, and play basketball second. I led with the words student and academics."

Robert reveals that 62 percent of graduating seniors at the Sports Academy went on to four-year university programs. Compare that to the 57 percent dropout rate at his former high school, Garfield, and you start to get a sense of what the future held for Robert. His radically different way of thinking about success for young people first became apparent here. The lengths he was willing to go to buck the system, just to give kids a chance, became obvious.

"In 1996, there were no girls' basketball leagues in East L.A.," Robert explains. "So I took my girls to play in the boys' leagues. We won half the games, even though the Police Activities League (PAL) coordinators, officials and coaches were not very welcoming to our female athletes."

Robert taught the girls on the basketball team many positive lessons by taking this step—to not shy away, to push the envelope, to go for what you believe in, to not take no for an answer, to take your punches and move forward. Robert always had the greater good in mind. A true leader, he stuck to his convictions and made it possible for the girls to compete. He refused to accept the unjust status quo. Around that time, he met a young woman named Gicel at a basketball camp at CSU-LA. She had been a basketball player and had won a championship at L.A. Wilson High. He hired her as a coach and they worked together at the academy. Gicel and Robert eventually married.

Robert fell in love with coaching sports and coaching kids. His success as the basketball coach earned him the program director position at the young age of 21. When Coach Hazzard became ill in 1997, the program began its decline and eventually lost funding. "Just when I figured out what I wanted to do, the program folded," Robert recalls. He returned to college, doing general coursework. Without a clear idea of what he wanted to do, he changed his major six times. His father was then diagnosed with cancer. Robert Senior had retired and was working with an affordable housing group called the Pico Union Housing Corporation. Robert helped him write grant proposals to raise funds for community redevelopment work. This volunteer work with his father would set the course for Robert's future.

About this time, the city of Los Angeles was knocking down many historical homes. Robert Senior found two beautiful craftsman homes built in 1902. He asked the owners if they would donate the homes to the organization for restoration and they agreed. He got the city community development office to lease two vacant lots in the downtown L.A. area. He passed away before the houses could be moved there. Because Robert Junior had worked with his father on this project, the Pico Union group asked him to help out after his father's death.

"I ultimately became Director of Development of the Pico Union Housing Corporation," he says. "I asked the Community Development Department for a $1.5 million grant to restore the homes. It was to be part of a YouthBuild program to teach young people construction skills and home restoration techniques." The Pico Union group received that grant just after Robert left the organization.

While at Pico, Robert attended college, hoping to graduate before his father passed. Unfortunately, the cancer had its own schedule. His father died in 2005. Robert graduated a year later. At the age of thirty, he received his undergraduate degree in interdisciplinary studies from CSU-Dominguez Hills. Thirty-year-old Robert now had his college degree, and two children. He also had experience in leadership, coaching, teaching, mentoring, grant-writing, interagency negotiations and relationship-building. He had attempted various educational ventures before finally succeeding. He knew the tenacity it takes to become a college graduate from East L.A. He also had that formative childhood memory of his father's community service work improving housing for the people. Yet fate had a hand in determining the course of life events.

• BA, Interdisciplinary Studies, CSU-Dominguez Hills

The Primer on Youth and Community Development Social Justice Organizations

At the intersection of community development work and social justice programs for youth is a U.S. Department of Labor-funded program called YouthBuild USA. LA CAUSA is part of this program. YouthBuild is "A youth and community development program that simultaneously addresses core issues facing low-income communities: housing, education, employment, crime prevention and leadership development. In the programs, low-income young people, ages 16-24, work toward their GEDs or high school diplomas. They learn job skills and serve their communities by building affordable housing, and transform their own lives and roles in society."

YouthBuild was started informally in 1988 and incorporated in 1990. This prominent program is equivalent in law to the Peace Corps and Head Start programs. The national network benefits from extraordinary public-private partnerships. It touts 273 programs in 45 states, Washington D.C., and the Virgin Islands. Since 1994, 92,000 students have built 19,000 units of affordable, increasingly green housing. [Source: www.youthbuild.org]

YouthBuild programs have provided experience and training for a variety of jobs within the green economy, including:

• Green building design and construction

• Home retrofitting for increased energy efficiency

• Solar and cool-roof installation

• Whole-home performance, including attic insulation and weatherization

• Environmental site assessment and sampling

[Source: See the YouthBuild Green Initiative brochure for complete list]

Three months after Robert graduated from college, a YouthBuild program position opened up in the city of Venice in western Los Angeles. Robert was quickly hired. He managed the program, worked with students and did the construction work with them. He got the daily interaction with people he had been missing. By now, Robert had worked in downtown L.A., East L.A. northeast L.A. and southern L.A. "But west L.A. was very different," Robert recalls. "The disparity between the 'haves' and the 'have-nots' was right in my face. My first day in Venice a limousine hit a homeless guy, and the limo driver got out to yell at the homeless guy."

While working in Venice in 2003, Robert met Alejandro Covarrubias, the founder of LA CAUSA. Robert was attracted to LA CAUSA's commitment to social justice, in addition to youth and community development. Robert shares, "I had always wanted to come home to East L.A. I wanted to work at LA CAUSA even though I was working at other places. I expressed my interest to Alejandro to be on his board."

Besides running LA CAUSA, Alejandro taught at several universities in Chicano studies departments. Four years later, Alejandro called Robert to tell him he was leaving LA CAUSA. He felt he had accomplished everything he had wanted to do there. He knew the community needed the organization to grow and it was time to hand the reins to a new director. "Alejandro asked me to consider replacing him as Executive Director," he shares. "There were two of us who interviewed. He recommended me because I was from the neighborhood and because I had a history of raising grant money."

Ironically, the board didn't think Robert had enough experience working with gang-affiliated kids despite having, as he says "every gang association within my own family." Due to his string of leadership roles, they perceived him as a suit-and-tie type of guy and didn't think the neighborhood kids would relate to him. They hired the other candidate. Robert told the board, "When it doesn't work out, please call me. I am still interested."

That call came six months later and Robert became the Executive Director of LA CAUSA. All told, there was a year-long transition between Alejandro leaving and Robert coming in. The turmoil scared the authorities at the Department of Labor who were funding the program. As a result, the program was almost defunded during the transition. The federal agency was also transitioning, from a HUD-managed program to one managed by the Department of Labor.

"We experienced a huge culture shock between HUD telling us we were a great program and Labor telling us we were a mess," Robert exclaims. "I was attracted to the challenge posed by the transition. I had mediated difficult challenges at a variety of organizations. I was good at it."

The myriad of challenges LA CAUSA tackles in East L.A. are enough to dissuade all but those with the thickest skins. Robert explains the fundamental, widespread problem that many adults in the area perpetuate. "My parents always talked about college to me," Robert states. "That is not happening in our neighborhood today. Many kids are still being told by parents and teachers that they are not fit for college."

The Many Facets of LA CAUSA

Walking around the expansive LA CAUSA facility in East L.A. is an extraordinary experience. One building houses a center run by former gang members and high school dropouts. These young men and women have become educated, certified professionals in green building techniques. They are leading the community's transformation from dilapidated homes to efficient, green homes run by solar power. They represent the most skilled green technicians LA CAUSA produces every year.

In another building, the College Career Center, a Sports Academy graduate applying to graduate school provides financial aid application advice to a LA CAUSA student who is wondering if she could really go to college. These seemingly disconnected parts are tightly interwoven to support LA CAUSA's complex mission.

"We found we needed to place our young graduates somewhere and there weren't many union jobs around. We began to think about placement possibilities. We started talking to them about green jobs. However, when they researched green jobs, they did not see 'solar installers,' the training we provide here. Instead, they saw 'engineers, architects and the like.' They realized that higher education was the true ticket to becoming a professional in the green economy. Those are the real, green, sustainable jobs."

LA CAUSA teaches the practice of greening homes and neighborhoods first, through hands-on construction skills using eco-friendly materials. The work empowers the kids first and shows them they are valuable citizens. They realize they can contribute to the community and that there are other ways to feel good about associating with people in the neighborhood besides gang affiliation. Later, many of these kids go on to college to learn the theories of sustainability and policy-making. The formula works.

Robert oversees many activities related to LA CAUSA's innovation and success. Let's look briefly at each of the parts, in case you decide to emulate Robert and create a similar organization in your community.

• **A Culturally-Relevant Education.** "An important difference between us and traditional high schools is this: there you have high expectations of students but low levels of support—thus the 57 percent drop-out rate. At LA CAUSA, we have high expectations and high levels of support. All 26 staff members are trained counselors and credentialed teachers. Nobody here is lost in a sea of 2,000 students. We are getting big and are starting to look at creating satellite schools. When people talk about high schools in East L.A., they talk about Garfield, Roosevelt and LA CAUSA. Kids are dropping out of the other two to come here—and our school's API scores are almost 150 points higher!"

Surprisingly not everyone in the community loves this successful youth development organization. When traditional institutions like public high schools fail and an alternative educational model succeeds, some teachers and administrators who are trying to perpetuate the status quo, however ineffective, get their feathers ruffled. You'll read that story later in this chapter.

- **Green Building Initiative (YouthBuild).** "The genesis of this initiative was that many homes here are in very bad condition. We started going into these homes and it was mind-boggling that people were living there. There were homes with huge holes in the floor. I remember a seven-month-old baby peeking into a huge hole in his living room floor. We started doing the rehab for these homes, reusing readily available construction materials, finding private money for this work."

- **Community Outreach.** "We do not have a contractor's license, so we cannot build for county- or city-funded projects. Instead, we take the community outreach role for these projects. We sell the community on the benefits of these green government programs. This way, the programs can actually be implemented and be successful because the people actually want them. This step is critical for our citizens to benefit from federal funds for greening low-income communities."

- **College Career Center.** "We have partnerships with local community colleges. Their faculty members teach classes here. From the first week of classes, we tell our students they are college students. Most of our kids have never imagined this possibility. When they visit our center to learn about college application and transfer processes, they are surrounded by college memorabilia. They start to actually feel like college students."

- **Summer Residency Program.** "About sixteen students each year attend the summer UCLA residency program. We pay $1000 per student for the week-and-a-half-long program. They live on campus and are taught by UCLA faculty. They learn about the college transfer process. They take extensive writing courses. They study the green economy and policy-making. There are classes on "Sustainability at UCLA" and "The History of Environmentalism in Los Angeles." They are in classes from 7 a.m. to 5 p.m. They are in study groups and writing papers until at least 10 p.m. We select peer mentors for them at UCLA. Then they are matched with a peer mentor from the graduate program for two years to help them navigate their way through the community college system."

- **Alumni Placement.** "Chris, from the construction team, was homeless for a while. Now he works here and wants to become an electrician. We were hiring for openings on our green team. He was super prepared for his interview. He researched green building techniques and his preparation floored me. When Labor Secretary Hilda Solis came to tour our facility, Chris gave the tour at the solar installation. He will be gone soon—different solar companies want to hire him already. Another of our graduates was hired by Willdan Energy Solutions. Because of his community outreach work here, he beat out college graduates for the position. He knows how to sell people on becoming greener. Other private sector companies know about LA CAUSA and our reputation. We are becoming a talent pipeline."

Now you see the complexity of projects and programs under Robert's leadership. How does a non-profit organization create new green jobs and what are those jobs? To answer this question, let's focus on two aspects of LA CAUSA's operations: the Green Building Initiative and the Community Outreach work.

Our federal government is doling out billions of ARRA dollars to communities across the nation. This money is intended to stimulate job growth and much of it goes to projects containing the word "green." LA CAUSA's experience is instructive for communities expecting to make major transformations using technologies perceived as new and strange by the residents they are intended to benefit.

LA CAUSA YouthBuild Green Building Initiative
LA CAUSA describes this initiative as, "…construction training as a means to offer youth concrete competencies that lend themselves to

addressing the deplorable housing conditions in their community, while providing them with a valuable skill set that can help young adults earn a living wage…We also teach green building practices including the use of recycled materials, low-toxic products and techniques to improve energy efficiency and water consumption." Robert believes that greening is what will save the community money, build the infrastructure and create jobs.

Alejandro Covarrubias, and LA CAUSA's Construction and Sustainability Manager Miguel Rodriguez, created this initiative and pushed to reuse existing materials.

Robert says, "It was an organic decision. It was how we were all raised. Reuse whenever possible. All of this was happening before I got here, before there was American Reinvestment and Recovery Act federal money. It was happening here before being green was sexy," says Robert.

Before joining LA CAUSA, Miguel worked in the Mexican communities of Oaxaca and Chiapas installing solar-powered systems and potable water sources. He led a fact-finding trip with LA CAUSA's leadership to see the methods being employed there and then helped to deploy the techniques in East L.A. Miguel says, "Our ancestors have been practicing so-called 'green' methods for thousands of years. This is not new. Through modernization, we've forgotten that. My grandparents in Mexicali lived in an adobe house. You can't beat that type of insulation. In Mexico, we use solar-powered systems not because it is 'green'—we use them because there is no electricity there."

The students learn hands-on skills at the headquarters training site and also at job sites. Members can earn a National Center for Construction Education and Research Certification. Many of the materials they use are made of recycled products and installed using the green building techniques learned in the coursework. The immediate result is modernized homes in East L.A. and residents who can live safely without fear of falling through their floors. The students learn about energy-efficient alternatives, Energy Star® appliances, drought-resistant landscaping and other techniques.

LA CAUSA students have rehabilitated sixteen homes, each with at least one greening project. LA CAUSA spends about $10,000 to rehabilitate a home in East L.A., including students' time and labor. The team has now "fully greened up" 33 private homes in the community. These homes have been transformed into green living showcases, with multiple projects completed in each one. Homeowners who will be offered these services down the road will need little convincing once they've seen a remodeled home. The community is beginning to understand what it means to green a home. They have seen the powerful impact of LA CAUSA's green team and that green housing can be created anywhere. See the inspiring LA CAUSA YouthBuild video that showcases work done at one home at www.lacausainc.org.

"It is very important to have green programs in this community. This is where greening makes the most sense," Robert states. "We have young people working on these projects who will walk down these streets every day. They will be able to say, 'I contributed to that home.' It is very meaningful."

Robert shares that even though these kinds of improvements make sense, educational outreach is needed to ensure residents understand and buy into the changes. "In the beginning, we would change all the appliances to new Energy Star-rated ones," Robert tells. "We would create a native garden of drought-resistant plants. Then we would go back later to visit the family and find the old refrigerator still sitting next to the new, efficient one. We would find the new native garden surrounded by water-sucking plants. We realized we needed to create the demand for greener solutions in the community and educate the residents to the benefits." This led to another job-creating engine, the community outreach work at LA CAUSA.

Community Outreach Jobs
for Government-Funded Greening Projects
Robert says that when people think of green jobs, they usually think only of construction workers and specialties like solar panel

installers. LA CAUSA is certainly creating those new jobs. The Wal-Mart Foundation, Weingart Foundation and Pentair Foundation have provided instrumental financial support by paying the salaries of LA CAUSA's alumni to do the construction work. "Nobody is talking about the outreach and education jobs being created by this community and housing greening activity," says Robert.

Robert explains why community outreach is a critical step that needs to be taken ahead of renovating homes with green building techniques and systems. "Last year, the county bid out a 22-home solar installation job," Robert explains. "We are tight with the community, so they hired us to do the outreach and organizing. However, solar power proved to be a tough sell in our community."

Why would anyone in a low-income community resist a free installation of solar panels on his or her home to save money? The answer provides a deep insight that this grassroots organization has into the culture and thinking of the neighborhood; insight that makes it a valuable partner in all community greening projects. It also makes it an effective model for other communities across the nation.

"We thought we would be able to give away solar panels to our community," Robert continues. "But many of these privately-owned homes are owned by seniors. Imagine trying to convince your grandmother to install solar panels on her home when she has lived 75 years without them. Also, they did not want county inspectors coming into their homes because there are illegal, non-permitted additions to many homes they do not want the county to see." Some homeowners were highly skeptical and asked questions like, "How do I clean the panels?"

LA CAUSA learned how much community education is required to make these types of projects work. Robert and his staff explained in Spanish the benefits of solar power. Eventually, they installed 21 of the 22 planned projects. This proved it was necessary to create and fund these critical new outreach jobs, so the community can be educated and sold on the technology and its benefits.

"The L.A. mayor's office has touted all the money they are going to spend on green projects. The missing link was the community organizing piece—the door knockers who sell the ideas to the community before anything can be built or improved." That indeed is what LA CAUSA does very well. Robert has actively advocated for these jobs to be created, and people are listening.

"Future projects will fund more people to do the door-knocking piece." The City of Los Angeles is now putting funds for outreach personnel into their RFPs (Request for Proposal) for different programs. It is a huge step forward, resulting in additional new jobs for each project. Without the community outreach step, similar projects may end up like many of the unsuccessful weatherization and solar programs attempted in L.A."

Are you interested in a career that focuses on creating greener, healthier communities? Find your community development director at your city hall and learn what community greening projects are being planned in your town or surrounding area. If the project sounds anything like what you read about here, ask the director if the RFP includes community outreach staff. If not, suggest to the director to add that function and explain the importance of it. Share this story of how LA CAUSA's team did successful community outreach, and how the project ultimately succeeded. Make the director think about how it could fail without doing the community outreach work first.

Does the project involve putting new technology, like solar panels, in or around private homes for energy efficiency? Does it sound like it would make a positive impact on residents yet they must first be sold on it? Will it involve low-income communities filled with skeptical people? Will there be a need for community outreach in another language? Propose that a community outreach team be formed to do this work and have it funded in the RFP. There is ample opportunity here to create a job for yourself if you take this unconventional approach!

If a project is already funded and underway, find out if it needs community outreach. If the project is stuck because of no outreach, perhaps you could organize a team to do that work. Could additional jobs be created for this and other similar projects in your community?

Alternative High Schools and Social Change

When Robert arrived at LA CAUSA three years ago, the organization serviced 50 to 60 students a year in its charter high school. Now, 130 kids enroll annually. The students earn 675 hours of community service each year. This earns them an AmeriCorps scholarship toward higher education.

All this success comes with a price when challenging the status quo. Robert and his organization have been perceived as a threat. They are succeeding where the local educational institutions have failed. He has received death threats from supporters of the local high schools! Real social change takes a tremendous amount of courage. "It has been tough," he says. "We have taken a lot of local heat for our education programs. All our students are high school dropouts. Years of educational reform at the federal level have really affected our kids in negative ways."

In a recent example, the kids of LA CAUSA wanted accountability and wanted to address the dropout problem. They asked tough questions and marched with signs that read "I am the 57 percent!" at the biggest football game in the community. They wanted to recruit students and alumni to address the problem head on. Instead, the march irritated the community. The proponents and creators of the status quo embarked on a campaign to create fear of change and fear of charter schools as new ideas were proposed.

Different community groups, high school students, school board members and teachers jockeyed for position when a new high school project was put out to bid. One idea called for a new five-school pilot campus to be built in the community, where no new schools had been built for over seventy years. The groups jointly supporting this idea were called the Collaborative, and Robert was part of it. He lobbied for that approach since he was a successful product of a small school, Garfield's own magnet school. His educational success there was perceived as a negative because it exposed the failure of the status quo. "The teachers were pissed," Robert relays. "They told the community members to go away. They asked 'What does the community know about running a school?'"

These events took Robert back to 1992, when he was on the shared decision-making council at Garfield. Once again, he was "the student" fighting the teachers to get lockers for the kids. He felt passionate about it. "For me, it was still my school. I took on this fight against the teachers at Garfield High. That is when it got ugly and I got those threats. As a result, teachers at Garfield that I grew up with no longer speak to me. What really hurt my heart was when the teachers in the Social Justice School at Garfield refused to sponsor the young people from the United Students Club, the ones advocating for educational options. The teachers held their affiliation with the Collaborative against them. The same students who organized to push for the first new school in decades lost their club's charter to meet on campus."

In the end, LA CAUSA was left out of the final discussions that ultimately resulted in positive change. Still, much learning happened for the kids of LA CAUSA. When Robert talks to his students, they realize they helped start the conversation at the football game. *They* made the legitimate argument for change and forced adults to take notice. *They* helped bring out the truth. Robert tells them they should be proud. Affecting real social change is not easy and it takes courageous, passionate leadership to succeed.

The new collaborative school, Esteban Torres High School, opened in the fall of 2010. It will be run by progressive Garfield High School teachers and others from the L.A. school district. Only time will tell if this approach, run by many of the same people who produced the 57 percent dropout rate, will create different results. They will have support from the community's organizations, so there is a great deal of hope. LA CAUSA will be there to catch those who drop out of any school. They will be there to provide renewed hope, education, training and leadership, so that more young peoples' stories can have positive endings and not end as statistics.

The Faces of Success

Earlier, I described six facets of LA CAUSA's operations. You have read about three of these so far. The other three are powerful evidence of success in a community that for too long has believed its children were not worthy of higher education. This organization is greening homes for families and educating disenfranchised youth, and also sending them to college. Yes, the very same kids who were pushed out of the local traditional high schools and written off by adult educators and counselors are now enrolled in college classes and succeeding.

College Career Center

In a community where few parents raising children have completed high school, the deck is stacked heavily against any child seriously thinking of applying to college. Their parents may have no idea what the college application process looks like or where to start. Add to that a 43 percent high school graduation rate and counselors who may not be accustomed to advising many kids to go to college, and you will quickly see why a free resource like LA CAUSA's College Career Center is a jewel in the community. The center is open to everyone who wants to receive advice on the college application process or other related processes. Each student is guided by a counselor who walks the student through the financial aid application steps. The College Career Center also takes on a variety of problems after the acceptance letter comes. Robert told me of a young man who got accepted into UC Santa Barbara, then ran into a $700 per month housing cost problem. He decided he could not go after all. The young people of LA CAUSA rallied and helped him get a scholarship. That young man now attends UCSB.

Robert introduced me to Denise Meda, a student applying to graduate schools, who was counseling another young woman on the college application process. Two young Latinas raised in East L.A. having this conversation is a success story in itself. Many conversations like this have now taken place in this facility and more will take place for years to come. I witnessed leadership, mentorship and life-changing advice occurring right in front of me. I wondered what the impact of such a powerful resource would have been during my own high school years. What if there had been college-educated Latinas available to talk to students in my own low-income community? How many more girls would have gone to college besides me? I was deeply moved by this place and by what it's doing for its young people.

Summer Residency Program at UCLA

Since the summer of 2009, sixteen LA CAUSA students have attended a UCLA summer residency program to learn about green careers and how to impact public policy. They are assigned peer mentors to work with them so they can eventually attend college. "There is one mentor there who got his GED while incarcerated, went to East L.A. Community College, and then transferred to UCLA," Robert tells us. "We show them that others have struggled and come out on top. These peer mentors are assigned to our kids for two years to assist them through the transfer process so they get into a university." It is a mind-boggling opportunity—kids who were once deemed un-teachable living on the UCLA campus and feeling what college is like. I asked Robert for examples of students who had attended the summer residency program in 2009, and to describe where they are now.

"A girl named Esmeralda from Van Nuys was valedictorian of LA CAUSA last year. She came by bus every day. She never missed a day despite dealing with transportation and housing issues. Esmeralda traveled more than ninty minutes each way, in L.A. traffic, to attend school. She wants to be a psychologist. She just finished her first year at Pierce College. She will be the first in our program to enroll in a university."

Another success story of this program is Moises Arrellana, the most affiliated gang member in 2009. Robert tells, "He was one of our best construction guys, although he struggled academically. He attended the UCLA residency program last summer. He struggled there too, but he visited a month later sporting a full head of hair. He looked and dressed differently. A change had happened. It was a very emotional moment for me. He then enrolled at East L.A. Community College. Due to family hardships, he had to work while attending college. LA CAUSA paid for him to get nine different certifications. He has a ton of new skills and strengths. That afforded him the opportunity to work in the oil clean-up efforts in Louisiana. He's now back at East L.A. Community College again, and taking a full load."

This is amazing success—changing and redirecting young people's lives, taking a gang member off the streets and putting him first on the path toward college and then *into* college. People are beginning to recognize these extraordinary results. In the summer of 2010, Robert and LA CAUSA were honored by CHCI as a leader in our green economy at the Latino Innovation Recognition session in Washington D.C. This is all possible because of the action, vision and leadership of people like Robert and Miguel, and the committed staff of this unique social justice organization.

The Motivation

Robert says that it is because of his father that he continues to do this work, "I'm supposed to be here. When my father took me to his community development office, I clearly remember seeing a pen holder on his desk. It was a carved, wooden fist, a symbol of the Chicano movement. One day, shortly after I arrived in this position here, I was at my desk. I saw a LA CAUSA poster in my office and looked carefully at our logo—a drawing of that same wooden fist." Serendipity perhaps?

Robert's father wanted the family to stay in the East L.A. community and to stay grounded in their culture.

"I want to do the same for my kids," said Robert. "I walk to work. I also argue with my wife because she wants our kids to attend private school. I want them to graduate from Garfield. Yes, I want the best for my kids, so I figure I've got about six years to improve Garfield High before my kids go there."

You can see that Robert's commitment to improving his community is quite personal. He also wants to change how people perceive East L.A. He wants people to understand the history of the culture, the social justice movement and its role in the civil rights movement.

"There is so much our kids do not know about our collective power and past leaders," Robert laments. "We do not think about Cesar Chavez and Dolores Huerta as leaders of the green movement, but they certainly were."

Robert has a clear vision for what he wants to create in East L.A.—a sustainable green community. He states, "There was never a demand for greening the community before our work started here. We have been creating community demand and doing the greening work since 2005 through the YouthBuild organization. This was long before there were federal dollars for being green."

What is next for LA CAUSA? Robert wants to green the commercial space in the community and teach business owners how to make their stores more energy-efficient and save money on their utility bills. He wants to transform the current "food desert" from a processed food-filled landscape into one filled with fresh produce. To do that, they must first change how people access food in the neighborhood. "We will create our own farmers' market at LA CAUSA." As they make their entire community healthier in nutritional, social, physical, environmental and educational ways, LA CAUSA will continue to add jobs to the community. It is currently adding fifty new jobs a year, and they are just getting started.

"We have created a do-it-yourself model for how to make a green sustainable community," Robert beams. "I think of it as a reverse trickle-down approach. We will force businesses to be more responsible for what they are selling to our people or we will stop buying from them."

Like any great social entrepreneur, Robert is focused on continuing to take action. "We are not waiting for the federal government to give us money and to create green jobs for us. We are pursuing and attracting our own funding sources to do it faster. We are very much responsible for green job growth year after year in both green building work and community outreach activity. Plus, in the last three years, we have also had *100 percent placement* in secondary education for our alumni."

There are many more success stories to be written. "In about five years, the young people who we helped get into college are going to start coming back as graduates," Robert forecasts. "They will have some serious ownership with our organization and will continue to evolve it. These are our future staffers, board members and community leaders. These are the people who will start their own organizations. I cannot wait for that day."

Robert Recommends

Robert's first advice to high school students who want to join the green movement in any capacity is this: "Get away from apathy." In other words, associate with people who care and want to contribute. Ditch the friends who are full of negativity and hopelessness. Build positive social networks. You must fight to play a larger role in the decision-making processes in your schools and communities.

For high school and college students, he offers these words:

"With non-profits, understand you will likely never be rich, but it is meaningful work. I learned from my dad that you must care deeply about your work. If you care about the environment, commit to public service. It is your civic duty. Identify your role in the community and work to empower your community. It's your duty to your neighborhood to become a success story."

"Start by learning about your community. *Just do something*. Learn who is doing what. Join in something that matters to you, and it will go from there."

There are 273 YouthBuild projects around the United States. Surely, there is one near you. It may not do everything that LA CAUSA does, but this organization is a fantastic starting point. Visit www.youthbuild.org to learn about this national youth and community development organization, the jobs it is creating nationally, and how to get involved or support it financially. If you know anyone who recently dropped out of high school, do them a favor and refer them to YouthBuild!

Here are some actions Robert recommends: To earn a powerful item for your resume while in high school or college, get your LEED Green Associate Certification. For a couple of hundred dollars, you can get this certification from the U.S. Green Building Council, the organization that created this internationally-recognized certification system. www.usgbc.org/DisplayPage.aspx?CMSPageID=2191

Look to the U.S. Green Building Council as the legitimate place to get informed on available LEED certifications offered by third parties. Avoid places that want to charge exorbitant fees to take the LEED Green Associate test and others. USGBC reviews the courses outside agencies offer. Check the course catalog of approved certification agencies at www.usgbc.org/coursecatalog/coursecatalog.aspx. They also have a free newsletter.

If you are interested in getting a solar installation certification, look to The North American Board of Certified Energy Practitioners (NABCEP). It is considered the "gold standard" for PV (photovoltaics) and solar thermal installation certification. www.nabcep.org

If you are interested in improving America's housing, check out the certification training offered by the Building Performance Institute (BPI). BPI is a "national standards development and credentialing organization for residential energy efficiency retrofit work." They are an independent, not-for-profit organization with a hands-on approach. www.bpi.org

Read the book by Van Jones: *The Green Collar Economy: How One Solution Can Fix Our Two Biggest Problems*, published by HarperOne in 2009.

Do community service. The following national organizations offer leadership development training and the chance to participate in service projects.

AmeriCorps: Put your ideals into action, get new skills and money for college. www.americorps.gov

Public Allies: I like their tagline: "New Leadership for New Times." www.publicallies.org

City Year: Young people give a year of full-time service, earning skills and opportunities to change the world. www.cityyear.org

Enterprise Community Partners, Inc: This large and established non-profit has the "ambitious goal of making sure every American lives in a decent, affordable home." It has more than 25 years of experience in the community development and affordable housing field. It provides capital and expertise. In East L.A. its people go through homes and award families solar panels, new water heaters, and so on. www.enterprisecommunity.org

College students can also make unique contributions to social justice and environmentally-focused, non-profit groups. Your status as an enrolled undergraduate or graduate student uniquely positions you to be a terrific mentor to kids who have struggled in life. Volunteer in some capacity as a mentor to high school kids in your community. Find out which groups in your community are serving kids like the ones you read about here. It is a powerful thing to do. You may decide to make a career of running an organization, serving on its advisory board or in some other capacity—you will never know what opportunities lie ahead unless you jump in to assist.

Robert recommends signing up for the free newsletter from the Green L.A. Coalition. One hundred organizations "doing anything green in L.A." have come together under this umbrella. The newsletter will also keep you informed about related events in the area. www.greenlacoalition.org (or through Facebook).

To read more about LA CAUSA in East L.A., see videos of its projects, student presentations and testimonials, visit www.lacausainc.org. You can support Robert and his staff in their amazing work by donating through this site.

For those making a mid-life career change, Robert recommends pinpointing what you are good at and love to do. What in your professional skills set drives you? Take that passion-based skill and pitch it to non-profit organizations in your community. Do you have financial skills to contribute? Marketing savvy? Are you good at acquiring donations? Do you love logistical challenges? Are you happiest when planning events? All these skills are vital to non-profit groups. Community organizations need all kinds of professional skills. Some may have the budget to pay you for the skills they need the most. For example, because Robert has built a track record as a man who can raise money, he has been asked to consult with other non-profit groups needing help writing grant proposals. This important work earns him extra cash and keeps him out there networking and meeting new people.

Robert suggests looking for short-term extension programs that universities offer in your area. In the L.A. area, UCLA has great sustainability programs. USC has a green office certification program. A word of caution: "You need to understand that most universities are not at this point yet. Be careful that, when you call around for green job training and education programs, you do not get sent to a vocational school. Many people do not understand what green jobs are!"

For one such program, Robert suggests looking at CSU-Dominguez Hills. It has an online distance learning program called Senior Certified Sustainability Professional.

The U.S. Green Building Council has an extensive Green Jobs Career Center. Many of the listings are for experienced professionals. Check it out at www.careercenter.usgbc.org/home/index.cfm?site_id=2643

Robert also encourages professionals in transition to volunteer. How did Robert get his grant-writing experience that now earns him consulting revenue for assisting with proposals? He wrote grants as a volunteer with his father at the Pico Housing Union Group. Remember how Robert started the conversation with the founder of LA CAUSA? He volunteered to serve on the board. Although he never got the chance to serve on that board, this put him in a favorable place in the founder's mind. When it was time to find a replacement, Robert got the call.

Robert teaching LA CAUSA students how packaged food travels to East L.A.
www.lacausainc.org

Frank Ramirez

Steel Mill or Stanford?
Creating Value with Ice and Energy Storage

"This green movement has the potential to create wealth
in ways I believe will be bigger than the Internet. The potential
is so huge that most people can't see it yet."
—Frank Ramirez, CEO of Colorado-based Ice Energy

$\mathcal{M}$y conversations with Frank Ramirez were part American history lesson, part too-amazing-to-be-true story, part primer on our nation's energy infrastructure and part semi-technical discussion about how air conditioning systems work. Above all, these conversations rank high up on my all-time list of informative and inspiring dialogues.

If you are interested in participating in the widespread movement to help our nation consume energy better and smarter, Frank wants you to know that there is money to be made along the way. You just have to understand some basic realities about how energy is produced, transported, stored and utilized today.

When you understand the extraordinary chain of events that made it possible for him to run a company creating never-before-seen energy storage solutions, you will likely see many different entry points for yourself. You may want to join in the national movement to create new energy efficiency and storage solutions after reading Frank's story.

The Boy in Colorado

In the small southern Colorado town of Pueblo, a Boy Scout leader approached a man and his son. Mr. Robinson, the scouting leader, asked Mr. Ramirez if his son, Frank, could join the local Boy Scout group. Frank's father responded that he did not have the money for such a thing. Mr. Robinson said, "We don't need your money. We just need your son." That is how young Frank, the oldest of the three Ramirez children, joined the Boy Scouts. Throughout the years, the troop found a way to keep him outfitted in camping equipment, despite his family's limited financial resources.

Frank Ramirez' parents were Francisco and Ana Maria Ramirez, an American-born man of Mexican descent and his Mexican immigrant wife. Francisco Ramirez, the man whose own father had died when he was a young child, had suffered from polio in his youth and used crutches.

Frank recalls, "For most of my early life, I recall my father traveling around town in what we called his putt-putt car—a motorized chair of sorts."

Francisco had struggled to complete his GED after Frank was born. He was limited to low-paying jobs in the community. To make additional money for his family, he sold matchbook advertising by going door to door to various businesses in his putt-putt chair. Although he had menial jobs, he always left the house in a pressed shirt that Ana Maria ironed for him.

Frank recalls, "He bought me a baseball glove after a month of selling those matchbook ads." Frank understood the effort his father had gone through to buy this gift. He cherished the glove as a sign of his father's love. His mother supplemented the family's income by making and selling tortillas. She also did laundry and ironing for neighbors. Frank learned that there is dignity in all work. He also learned that the way you present yourself to others truly matters.

"We learned how to do what we had to do," Frank says. "I never knew we were poor. I only learned that later in my life. My mother only looked at the many blessings we had. We were not focused on what we did not have."

Frank recalls the role of religion in his young life. "We were people of great faith. I recall our solemn nighttime visits to the Knights of Columbus round-the-clock vigils at church. I remember my dad struggling down to his knees during the Mass, but he knelt."

When Frank was fifteen years old and had been in Scouting for several years, he promised his father he would become an Eagle Scout—the top rank. A few weeks later, Francisco suddenly died of a massive heart attack. Shortly after Francisco's death, Ana Maria lost most of her eyesight to an aggressive form of macular degeneration. Although she could barely see, she continued to bring in money for the family doing the same work in the community.

Frank recalls, "She never lost a step in blessing my sister, brother and me with unconditional love and plenty of wisdom in stories, songs and *dichos* (sayings). She reminded us that anything is possible with faith, education and hard work."

Living in the huge void left by his father's passing, and his mother's adjustment to blindness, Frank persevered through high school and excelled. He was on track to graduate in the top two percent of his class. He also continued working to fulfill his promise to his father and became an Eagle Scout.

Frank's high school counselors recognized his exceptional all-around talents. In similar situations, guidance counselors would likely direct the young man to apply to a top university or at least a state college. They would coach the student to complete financial aid applications. They would discuss options for higher education to fulfill the potential they saw in him. But none of those things happened for Frank as a high school senior. Instead, he was slotted to work in the local steel mill, because the counselors believed it was best for his family. You can see why. With a deceased father, a blind mother and two younger children in the home it made sense to put the practical needs of the Ramirez family on Frank's shoulders. In the minds of the guidance counselors, the responsibility to support the family fell squarely on Frank—they saw no other option. They meant well.

Frank approached his senior year in relative ignorance. For others in Frank's situation, things would happen as envisioned by the guidance counselors. The young man would start working at the mill a few weeks after the excitement of the graduation ceremony. He would dutifully support his mother and siblings because that is what others expected. Nobody would ask what he wanted to accomplish for himself, because it did not matter. The young steel mill employee would become a middle-aged steel mill employee. Decades later he would retire, unless the mill closed suddenly. But Ana Maria's lessons of fate and faith would prove true for her son. Fate would intervene and steer him thousands of miles from that steel mill.

A Cascade of Events

During the spring of his senior year, Frank entered a *Readers Digest-* sponsored public speaking contest for Eagle Scouts. "The Boy Scouts of America is the only youth organization that provides an annual report to Congress," Frank explains. "I won the local public speaking contest and the right to represent my state in the Western Regional competition."

The Region 8 contest was held in Kansas City, Kansas. Frank recalls, "I had never been on an airplane before. I flew to Kansas with my guitar. It gave me a sense of security. I did not even have a complete Eagle Scout uniform until I won the contest. There was a frenzy of activity to get me completely outfitted for that trip. I started to realize that we were indeed *pobres* (poor people)."

In Kansas City, Frank won the regional competition. Many people were seeing his excellence and potential. They only saw Frank, knowing nothing of Frank's family situation in Pueblo.

"I was appointed to be a 'Report to the Nation Scout.' There is no higher honor for an Eagle Scout." He had fulfilled his promise to his father—and then some! Future Pueblo steel mill employee Frank Ramirez was on his way to our nation's capital to brief the Speaker of the House and the President of the United States on Scouting in America.

According to the Boy Scouts of America (BSA), "The BSA operates under a charter granted by the U.S. Congress. One requirement is the annual report on the achievements of the Scouting program. The delegation of Scouts will present the report to the Speaker of the House as required by the charter. Every U.S. president since William Howard Taft has received a BSA Report to the Nation delegation. Each U.S. president serves as an honorary president of the BSA during their term in office." [Source: www.bsartn2008.org]

The "Report to the Nation" designation for a scout is a big deal. The handful of young people chosen to give the report to our national leaders represents millions of Scouts. This is a huge privilege. Frank joined the group of other regional representatives and attended this whirlwind ten-day trip to our nation's capital.

"I visited President Richard Nixon in the Oval Office," Frank shares. "I presented him with a gift. It was a proof casting of a set of Norman Rockwell silver medals depicting Boy Scouts doing good deeds. I have a photograph of me presenting these medals to our President."

Are you thinking what I'm thinking? There is no way this young man is headed for the steel mill after high school graduation.

Frank continues, "I met one-to-one with George Meaney, the leader of the AFL-CIO. I met the man leading the FBI, Mr. J. Edgar Hoover. I would later learn that the photograph of me with Mr. Hoover was the last picture taken of him before he passed away shortly after our visit."

Frank was then selected as one of three scouts to be on *The Today Show* with Barbara Walters in New York City. Frank says, "There I was on national television getting peppered with questions about Scouting. My mother back home got to hear me on the television talking to Barbara Walters."

His mother and his Pueblo community must have been incredibly proud. Imagine what his father would have said if he had lived to witness this moment.

Frank recalls, "I was eighteen. This trip opened my eyes to a world of opportunities I had only read about. The people and places we visited were extraordinary." The experience had a deep impact on him.

"At the Waldorf Astoria Hotel in New York City, I remember being shocked by everything," he states. "On the menu, a slice of Rocky Ford cantaloupe was priced at $1.50. I found that outrageous when an entire cantaloupe back home sold for a nickel."

It was at this posh Park Avenue hotel that fate would make her strongest intervention. "At the Waldorf, I was speaking with a Scouting leader. He asked me if I had plans after high school. Specifically, he asked if I was going to college. I told him I wanted to go to college. He asked me where I had applied. I told him I had not applied anywhere and I did not know how to apply."

The Scouting leader was surprised and said, "You are at the top of your class. You are President of your Student Leadership Council." Frank recalls that the leader listed other achievements he knew Frank had accomplished.

"I again told him I had not applied anywhere and he left it alone," Frank remembers. "You have to realize that nobody in my family had ever completed high school. There was no legacy of going to college or of even knowing how that happened."

The ten-day, East Coast tour of national treasures and meeting national leaders came to an end. Frank tells us, "When I returned to Pueblo after that trip, and as a result of the national press exposure I received, there were applications from both Harvard and Stanford universities waiting for me. Along with the applications were letters informing me that they were allowing me to apply late since the deadlines had passed. Also included was information about potential full-ride scholarships. Apparently someone in the Scouting hierarchy had made some phone calls."

This is the power of a personal network. For many young people in America, including me, whose immigrant parents never applied to college, the high school guidance counselor provides the spark and know-how to pursue higher education. However, for a boy with a deceased father, whose counselors with all the best intentions were guiding him toward the mill, fate had to intervene in the form of a national Scouting leader at the Waldorf Astoria in New York City.

Education, Work and More Education

Frank completed his college applications and forms for scholarships. He eventually received admission and a full scholarship to attend Stanford University. He majored in economics.

"I chose economics because I received a C grade in my first economics class there," he remembers. "It was the first time I had ever received anything but an A or a B in a class. I was disgusted by it. I felt I had to beat it, so that is why I chose that major." Apologetically he says, "It is not very scientific or inspirational."

Motivation comes in many different forms. The important thing is that he received his undergraduate degree from Stanford University, something that no one had ever imagined as an option for him. Frank shared that his original dream was to earn a law degree and follow in the footsteps of Frank Evans, his Representative from the 3rd Congressional District in Pueblo.

"I wanted to leave the world a better place for my having been here," Frank states. "I believed that public service held the key."

He applied to the University of California at Berkeley's Boalt School of Law.

"My rather naive perspective of public service was shattered after living one summer in the home of the sitting Senator Walter Mondale of Minnesota," he shares. "I learned of the numerous tradeoffs in running for and serving in an elected capacity. I decided instead to become a judge."

Law school opened a new window into the world of corporate finance and securities. After graduating with his law degree, Frank headed for Washington D.C. as a cub attorney with the Securities and Exchange Commission. There he peered into a world which, until that time, he had known about solely from course work and reading *The Wall Street Journal.* He was smitten. Next, he was accepted to the Graduate School of Business at Stanford University to pursue his MBA.

- BA, Economics from Stanford University
- JD, Boalt Hall School of Law, University of California, Berkeley
- MBA, Graduate School of Business at Stanford University

Entering the Energy Sector

After receiving his MBA, Frank became a managing director for the Wall Street firm, Bear Stearns. He later founded a boutique derivatives group inside Alex Brown & Sons. He invested in a few private companies before co-founding his current company, Ice Energy.

Where and when did Frank's interest in the energy sector begin? "I didn't have an epiphany. I didn't have an 'ah-ha!' moment. It came to me as I explored a business idea," says Frank. He had co-founded a company named Endure to develop on-site power for mission-critical processing of critical data.

"We believed there was a growing need for secure environments to mine and process data," Frank explains. "These intensive processing activities would require a high degree of security and a high level of electrical power." While pursuing this business idea he learned about our nation's antiquated energy infrastructure.

"I learned our energy infrastructure was built after the Korean War in the 1950s," Frank says. "I learned it had been operated with minimal investment over the decades. It was adequate to provide the everyday power to homes but it was not robust enough to provide clean, uninter-ruptible power to these data processing facilities. The infrastructure would be insufficient for the facilities we imagined. That's where I learned about the inefficiencies of generation and transmission."

America's Attitude Toward Energy

Like most Americans, Frank grew up believing that energy was available in an unlimited supply, to be consumed as much as possible.

"I vividly remember the marketing posters at the utility company where we paid our bill. They featured Reddy Kilowatt, a cartoon character of vaguely human form with lightning bolts for a body, a light-bulb for a nose and electrical sockets for ears," Frank recalls. "Reddy Kilowatt encouraged us to use electricity as our servant to wash and dry our clothes, cook our food, wash our dishes, and heat our homes. There was but one objective behind those programs—to get Americans to consume electricity without limit."

Then we experienced the 1970s oil crisis. Oil became very expensive. We saw on TV the miles-long lines of cars waiting to fill up at gas stations. Suddenly, we all wanted energy efficiency. This was the national sentiment as long as oil was perceived to be scarce and prices remained high. Then oil prices dropped precipitously and we as a nation dropped any real efforts to pursue efficiency or to explore alternative energy sources.

"Historically we have spoken about conservation, doing less with less. But as an American people, we have difficulty being told to do without. We are a privileged people. We are used to getting what we want when we want it. In the '70s when the price of oil dropped to $25 per barrel, we forgot that we had a long-term problem to solve through efficiency because power was again inexpensive," says Frank.

I inquired why he thinks it is different this time around in the 21st century. Why is energy efficiency really important to us as a nation now? Why are we finally really researching and implementing alternative energy sources?

Frank says, "The September 11 attacks accelerated our desire to minimize our dependence on imported fossil resources. Couple that with our understanding of the need to decrease our carbon emissions, and you see that a real change in attitude has happened. The attacks convinced us finally that we need to find a different way. We can indeed begin to lessen our dependence on oil from countries that would seek to do us harm. We understand now the need to increase attention on renewable, sustainable means of fueling our lifestyle."

We must not repeat the mistakes of the '70s. Frank believes that this time, we as a nation are finally serious about energy efficiency and renewable resources. There is a great deal of low-hanging fruit to pick as we transform our physical energy infrastructure and reinvent how we power our nation this century. Frank sees many opportunities.

Frank believes that, "Nowhere does a greater opportunity exist today than in the chance to create value from the many changes that are occurring in the energy markets."

Fully appreciating what Ice Energy has created first requires a basic primer on the elements of our national electrical grid infrastructure. It is important to understand some key points about electricity generation, distribution and transformation. This basic understanding is absolutely foundational knowledge for future entrepreneurs wishing to reduce how our nation consumes energy. I will provide a brief primer here based on what I learned from Frank. At the book's companion website, you will find a much longer, *unabridged* version of this chapter. There you will find more depth on the industry and more about the inefficiencies of the status quo. You can also explore the resources provided at the end of this chapter.

The Primer on Our Electrical Grid

Frank believes Americans have become over-dependent on electricity—and complacent. "We don't think twice about consuming electricity for comfort," he states. "Nowhere is this truer than when we flip on the AC switch."

To meet this demand, our utility companies have built out the necessary generation, transmission, and distribution resources to assure that electricity is ever ready at the flip of that switch. Since demand for electricity varies wildly between the peak of the late afternoon and the valley of the late evening, we average less than fifty percent utilization. It's like owning a fully-equipped, fully-staffed automobile factory that can produce 2,000 cars a day, yet ninety percent of the time you're content to only produce 1,000 cars per day. In other words, we are intentionally overbuilt and underutilized to avoid blackouts on the most demanding days. Think of our existing electrical infrastructure as an expensive and environmentally unsound contingency plan. This continues because we, as a nation, have become smug about how we get our electricity.

For example, if you have ever been in the California Central Valley when it is 106 degrees, you know exactly what Frank means by "peak period." On extremely hot days nearly all the air conditioning systems in the state are running. The draw on California's electrical grid is tremendous and has led to "rolling brown-outs" and "rolling black-outs." This is a set of procedures the utility companies put into place to meet increased demand on these extremely hot days. They shut down sections of the grid in one part of the state to divert power to, for example, the city of Fresno where most of the city's AC systems are running. But what about the days when it is not 106 degrees? Frank points out, "We are using the infrastructure that we have less and less—not more. This is not efficient."

That said, how do wind power and solar power figure into the equation? Frank understands that many environmentalists focus on these alternative energy sources, which is good—to a point. However, he wants us to grasp some key points about alternative sources.

"These sources are intermittent and variable," he explains. "Wind power happens when it happens and the wind can suddenly stall. Wind also has a tendency to blow the strongest at night and rarely blows at all when it is hot. The sun, of course, is only around for half the day. Solar photovoltaics reach highest output at mid-day, yet system demand peaks between 4:00 and 6:00 p.m. Thus, wind output does virtually nothing to address the peak; solar is only partially helpful but not helpful when clouds roll overhead."

Wind and solar are clean sources of energy, yet they do not work continuously round-the-clock. Nor can these sources be scheduled to address the all-important peak demand.

Frank continues, "The big lie we are being told is that our energy prices will go down as we harness new renewable sources of energy. It's a lie, because even with these new sources, we will still need the big iron infrastructure in place today, running primarily on coal and gas, to insure the lights stay on when the variable resources fail to produce. The addition of distributed renewable resources will, however, increase the difficulty for utilities to manage the reliability of the system."

As a case in point, he describes a situation in California. More wind energy is produced at night than is actually demanded by customers needing overnight electricity. Therefore to get users for the wind energy being produced (because it cannot be stored), the Cal Independent System Operator (ISO) is paying commercial customers to take wind power on at night. It's like the utility company is saying, "Here, we produced this clean wind power. Can we pay you to use it right now? Please?" This is absurd and results in a net negative revenue situation. This practice is unsustainable, yet many people in our culture are excited about sexy, new, clean energy sources. Still, the real problem of storing and using this clean wind energy remains.

"We cannot depend on these sources to be there at the moment the energy is needed. Storing the energy these sources produce becomes critical if it is to be used to its highest value. Clean, efficient, and cost effective storage of energy provides one of the largest opportunities for creating value. Storage is the missing leg of the horse in the nation's energy policy. We do this with all other commodities to better match demand and supply. We can store water, money, food, oil reserves and the like. We need to do the same with alternative energy generation." Future entrepreneurs who want to create clean energy solutions should ponder this question: How can we *store* clean energy produced from a variety of sources when it is generated before the time we need to power something?

Creating ways to store electrical energy has never been a national priority. This is changing, however, in part due to the leadership of California's Attorney General and Governor, evidenced by the passage of AB2514 in 2010—the nation's first measure directed specifically at increasing energy storage on the electrical grid. We have developed a national consumption mentality and become accustomed to generating, distributing, transmitting and using energy when we need it. America traditionally does not have a saver's mentality—creating energy and *storing* it for later use. We generate and consume—and don't save—largely because most people do not think energy can be stored. You need people like Frank to come along and think differently about such complex problems.

"Energy storage provides the means to help deliver on the promise of variable and renewable resources by helping to firm up their value," he states.

Frank explains, "My entire career has been devoted to extracting complexity premiums from markets that are in transition. [This means he steps into the chaos when things are changing, works to understand the situation and creates economically valuable solutions.] I have worked where there are high communication costs because people simply do not understand each other. [This means he sifts through the jargon and synthesizes the critical information that all players need to understand in order to work together to solve a problem.] Here is where there is a great opportunity to create wealth by improving communication. The difficulty in the energy industry—and the cooling industry—is there is a lot of different jargon. Most of the jargon is not understood by participants in the different industries involved. There are entire sectors that need to be working in conjunction with each other, but they do not even share a common language to discuss problems, much less to develop solutions for efficiency."

Our national problems of energy creation, energy efficiency and energy storage cannot be solved if all the players are speaking past each other in different jargon. An example of these high "language transaction costs," as Frank likes to say, is the language of energy efficiency and the different units used by different players to talk about it. This brings us to a short, important lesson.

Basics: Electrical Generation, Transmission, Distribution

The process of converting fossil fuels such as coal and natural gas into electricity is surprisingly wasteful. In fact, the electrical generators at coal and oil-fired plants operate with a typical efficiency of only 33 percent. It is only about 50 percent for combined-cycle, gas-fired plants. [Source: *Electrical Generation Efficiency*—Working Document of the NPC Global Oil & Gas Study, 18 July 2007]

Incredibly, more than sixty percent of the heat generated during the combustion process (fuel-burning) is lost. That means only forty percent of it can ever become useful electrical power. It gets worse when it is hotter; higher temperatures mean lower efficiencies. Plus, there is more loss through the wires and transformers that move the electricity to our offices and homes. Finally, the efficiency rating of an appliance like an air conditioner is about 72 percent. Therefore about 80 percent of the mechanical work that might be performed by combusted fossil fuel is lost to waste heat. We call that electrical system efficiency—or should we say inefficiency. [Source: Sherwin, Elton B. *Addicted to Energy: a Venture Capitalist's Perspective on How to Save Our Economy and Our Climate*, Energy House Publishing, (2010)]

Have you ever touched a wire, like your laptop cord, and found it warm to the touch? That is thermal inefficiency. Our entire electrical system is thermally inefficient. The demand for electricity peaks during the hottest days of the summer when we turn on our air conditioners or head into the shopping malls to seek comfort from the sweltering heat. Frank reveals that air conditioners typically operate at night with 87 percent efficiency while daytime efficiency drops to about 72 percent. Therefore when it is 100 degrees outside and we need our air conditioning systems to keep us cool and comfortable, these systems are operating at their absolute worst efficiency. They are also consuming energy from the generation plant at its worst efficiency, and transmitting the energy over the wires at their worst efficiency. That is the reality of our system.

Generating, transmitting and appliance usage efficiencies improve when it is cooler outside. Electrical efficiency is better during cool nights. The enormous losses of source energy required to generate daytime cooling paints a bleak picture of our grid's inefficiencies. The stage is set for energy storage solutions.

Tackling such complexity begins with a question: *what if we could produce, transmit and store electricity at night?* Electricity can be generated more cleanly and efficiently at night and costs less to produce. This creates a great economic opportunity.

The Company and its Coolest Solution

Far from his mother's beloved Michoacan, Mexico, warm land of the *aguacate*, (avocado), and his father's native Jalisco, Frank is creating clean energy solutions and innovating with ice.

"We are leveraging the efficiencies that are made available to us every day by the simple rotation of the planet. The relatively cooler temperatures that exist in the late evening and early morning provide a powerful thermal advantage to store energy in an efficient manner."

Freezing water to make it into ice provides the perfect medium to store energy. Water is renewable and not harmful to the environment. Melting ice to water releases the same amount of energy that it takes to bring water at room temperature to the boiling point. Among other things, Ice Energy allows energy-hogging air conditioners to have much lower energy requirements while using electricity that is produced, transmitted and distributed cleanly and efficiently.

Frank co-founded Ice Energy with Greg Tropsa and Brian Parsonnet. These three entrepreneurs have a passion to protect the environment and understand the problems associated with the country's power plants. Together with friends, they kicked in the first capital and sweat equity to start the company. Ice Energy has time-shifted the production of energy needed for AC, the most demanding system on the grid, by "rejecting heat from water to make ice at night" using the company's Ice Bear® product. This ice then provides the juice needed to run the AC during the day. It circulates chilled, ice-cold refrigerant from the tank to the installed AC system. This means the energy-intensive AC compressor can be off during peak daytime hours when the grid is least efficient. Extraordinarily, thousands— perhaps millions—of AC systems can now avoid sucking electricity during daytime periods of extreme temperatures. See how it works by watching the video at www.ice-energy.com.

Ice Energy is doing something that most believe is impossible. It is difficult for people to appreciate the idea of electrical energy storage. The North American Electric Reliability Corporation (NERC), states "Unlike water or gas, electricity cannot be stored. It must be generated as it is needed, and supply must be kept in balance with demand." [NERC source: www.nerc.com/page.php?cid=1|15]

Frank says, "We are working with traditional generating resources. We are improving the conversion of fuel through cooling and boosting efficiency by as much as fifty percent. It is done by understanding and leveraging all of the inefficiencies that exist across the system that often are not exploited because they are not understood."

This innovative solution is designed for highly-scalable deployments by utility companies, not just at individual commercial sites. In a press release announcing one of several awards, Ice Energy stated, "When deployed in scale by utility companies, our solution represents an important change—from just looking at site energy efficiency to unlocking the tremendous potential for savings from integrated energy system efficiency, from generation, transmission and distribution to the point of delivery and consumption at the building."

Frank explained further, "We now have a proven system that is not only cost-effective and reliable, but also supports our utility's environmental initiatives with reduced carbon emissions, the integration of intermittent renewables such as wind and solar, and clean energy storage."

What is Frank's motivation to apply his talents to this particular endeavor? "There's finally recognition that we have abused the stewardship of what we have been given. As Americans, we love energy efficiency because it means we can do more with less. We do not necessarily like doing less with less (conservation), but doing more with less definitely appeals to our aspiring nature. I love being part of the movement that is asking the right questions, so that our progeny have a healthy planet to raise their own children."

He says about Ice Energy, "I love what we are doing not only because we can do well for our shareholders, but also because we are doing good for our planet. We truly are doing more with less energy. We are providing superior comfort while using fifty percent less fuel to do it."

About ongoing sustainability efforts and different approaches, he states, "It may be possible to work on changing consumer behavior. For example, one way to go about it is to say to consumers 'please take on some personal discomfort for the good of our country and planet.' We've shown we can do it for short periods of time. However as a people, we have dreams and aspirations that force us to do otherwise in the long term. That's why it is more important to create new ways to responsibly leverage the resources we have. We can get there without sacrificing economic growth and personal comfort, but we will have to be intelligent in using technology so we can achieve these efficiencies while reducing our footprint."

"This work at Ice Energy is good for our planet," he shares. "It is inspirational. We have been able to attract extraordinary people.

Our company is a great platform for learning how to leverage intellectual and financial capital to solve old problems with new ways of thinking."

Frank says potential investors have asked him, "Please tell me again why you do not have any competitors?" It is hard for conventional thinkers to wrap their minds around the idea that something marketable is so original, that it is the only one of its kind. Frank tells them, "You can invest in us because we are the innovators or you can wait a few years to invest in those that will eventually learn about us and become our competitors."

This is an exciting time for Ice Energy. It is attracting new investors and recently secured significant new funding. The company has expanded its executive team. This is a privately-held company creating a new sector in clean energy and positioned for phenomenal growth.

Frank is quite aware that there was a time in his life, and a family situation, when all of this almost didn't happen. I asked him if he ever thinks about how he might have missed all this by going to work at the steel mill. I asked if he thinks about the boys, turned men, who are still working at that mill today. He answered that indeed he thinks about that often and that he is humbled.

What Matters Most to Frank—Besides His Company
Frank is a walking inspiration to young men, to entrepreneurs and to all Latinos. He has specific advice for those interested in joining the movement toward better stewardship of our fossil fuels. But before we end with his sage and specific advice, it is worth taking a moment to see what Frank does when he is not in CEO mode. How is he giving back to the organization that made his early success, and ultimately his current life, possible?

In our conversations, the Boy Scouts of America always came up. The promise to his father to achieve the rank of Eagle Scout put Frank in a place to meet the person who helped him see a bigger vision for his life— a national leader in the BSA intent on making a difference. Today Frank is a national leader of the BSA. He is doing for today's young men what was done for him. He is passing on the values of the Boy Scouts, living by those values and being a visible role model. Frank is president of his local Boy Scout Council in Northern Colorado, providing leadership in his home state. He is active on the National Executive Board and serves on the Hispanic Initiatives Committee headed by Ralph de la Vega. Frank beams when he reveals that both of his boys are Eagle Scouts, and both are now studying at Stanford "growing in knowledge and wisdom."

Within the BSA, Frank has a specific goal. "We must provide this mechanism of character and values-based development to our young men, especially young Latinos in communities that have no legacy of Scouting," Frank relays. He is helping to reach Latino families in culturally relevant ways. One of Frank's favorite sayings is: "*El que se acerca a un árbol macizo, buena sombra lo cobija*"—He who gets close to a solid tree will be covered by great shade. It is all about associating with the right influences. The strong tree provides the best shade; the weak tree provides none at all. It is your choice where to stand.

Frank is using his ability to lead and think differently in organizations in transition, with the goal to expand the number of Latinos in the Boy Scout ranks. Earlier Frank said, "I have worked where there are high communication costs because people simply do not understand each other." There is a potential language barrier to overcome when trying to convince parents to let their kids try Scouting. Plus, the message and words matter. Telling parents you are taking their kids camping does not work with Hispanic parents that tend to be very protective of their children. I know this from first-hand experience; my mother almost did not let me join the Girl Scouts because of the camping thing! It's a non-starter and Frank understands that. Instead, the BSA now goes to soccer fields and invites entire families to familiar, family-style outings (*un día de campo*) to introduce them to the values of Scouting.

This new approach at the BSA spearheaded by Frank is sheer brilliance, kind of like using ice to run air conditioning systems. Another complex problem solved by the mind of someone willing and able to understand the complexity swirling around it. When he goes into these communities, he tells them that their associations will define them. In another example of a great *dicho*, Frank tells the young boys, "*Dime con quién andan y te diré quienes serán.*" Tell me who you hang out with and I will tell you who you will become. I recommend that you find someone like Frank to associate with quickly.

Ice Energy has received many awards and significant industry recognition for its breakthrough innovations. Among these awards are the:

• Green Building Innovation Award: A panel of judges representing the American Society of Heating, Refrigeration and Air Conditioning Engineers made this selection.

• *Buildings Magazine's* "Top 100 Products"

• California Energy Commission's "Flex Your Power Award"

• "Cool Vendor" by Gartner, Inc.

As a young man, Frank boarded his first airplane with his guitar in hand. It provided him a sense of comfort on the trip that ultimately changed his life. The guitar he is holding now, the instrument of action and power, is his executive leadership of a company innovating ways to improve the efficiency and reliability of our nation's electrical infrastructure. Frank demonstrates that the intersection of business aspirations and environmental advocacy is a terrific, potentially lucrative place to apply your talents. Here you can truly make a positive impact on our nation's resource utilization while improving our energy efficiency.

Advice from the CEO
For further insight, Frank recommends:

- Learn about the innovative Ice Bear products that are vastly reducing energy requirements for AC systems. Visit Ice Energy at www.ice-energy.com.

- Gain a deeper understanding of the national electrical grid, its inefficiencies and limitations plus where improvements are needed. www.smartgridtoday.com

- See a concise graphic called "Understanding the Grid." Definitions of reliability concepts, terminology and technical reports are also available for the most curious minds. www.nerc.com/page.php?cid=1|15

- Learn about the values of Scouting and its benefits to our young people: www.scouting.org

Frank offers this advice for high school students who want to reduce our energy consumption and prepare to work in the clean tech economy.

"High school students should make a special effort in science classes to go beyond the basic principles learned in school. Engage your teachers to take your book learning and apply it outside of the classroom. For example, the first law of thermodynamics says that energy can neither be created nor destroyed—it merely changes form. This is a perfect backdrop for recycling and reusing initiatives. Why should we bury cans or glass when it takes less energy to reshape the material into new cans or glass items than to extract the raw materials to form them from scratch?"

For college students who want to work in this industry now, or to prepare to work in the clean tech economy, Frank offers:

"I recommend that college students read as much as they can to find an area that sparks an interest. Good online places to begin include:

- www.matternetwork.com

- www.news.cnet.com/greentech

- www.solveclimate.com/blog

- www.earthtechling.com

- www.cleantechies.com

- www.brighterenergy.org

For professionals in mid-career transition wishing to enter the clean tech economy, Frank offers this advice:

"On the jobs and career front visit www.greencareersguide.com and find the books section. Several books here might be of value, including the familiar "for Dummies" version and others. Also please see the sub-sites within that website too, like these:

- www.greencareersguide.com/How-to-Find-Green-Jobs-Training.html

- www.treehugger.com/files/2009/01/careers-renewable-energy.php

"In addition, there are a number of interesting and informative sites that are good places to start, including:

- www.greenbiz.com

- www.environmentalleader.com

- www.sustainablebusiness.com

"Also, check out the *Clean Tech Job Trends Report 2010*." This report, issued by Clean Edge and sponsored by Deloitte, highlights major trends that are reshaping the clean tech jobs landscape in the United States and globally. According to the report's description, "clean energy continues to fuel the plans of many cities, states, nations, investors, and companies as they look for the next wave of innovation and growth. The report provides key insights and analysis of the most important employment trends globally—making it a 'must read' for job seekers and decision makers." Download the report at: www.cleanedge.com/reports/reports-jobtrends2010.php.

Company-owned photo by Michael Lewis

Frank with Ice Bear unit—putting clean energy to work in the form of ice
www.ice-energy.com

Final Thoughts:
Objectives, Insights and Opportunities

*W*hen I started these interviews, I was simply writing a feature article for *Hispanic MBA*, the magazine of the National Society of Hispanic MBAs. In my pitch I told the publisher I was curious to answer a question in my mind: "As our green economy picks up momentum, what role if any, is the Latino business community playing?"

To write that article, I created a questionnaire to quickly interview thirteen people, most of whom I had never met. The questionnaire was designed to probe just deep enough to write the article. With the exception of Frank Ramirez, who gave me two and a half hours of his time to provide a verbal primer on our national electrical grid, these initial interviews were completed in about an hour each.

That 3000-word feature article was published in the fall of 2009 as NSHMBA's national membership gathered in Minneapolis for the association's national conference. I attended and spoke with my fellow NSHMBA members. I heard, "Great article but I want to know much more about each of these people." So did I!

So began my quest to write this book. My objectives all along have been two-fold:

1. Educate our high school and college students and our in-transition job seekers on different industries undergoing transformation to the emerging green economy. It is a complete rethinking of the status quo. These are the industries where innovations, companies and jobs are being created today and for at least the next decade.

2. Elevate the nearly-invisible success of today's educated Latino innovators and business leaders into the consciousness of mainstream America. I want to change the media conversation and imagery surrounding today's American Latinos away from immigration/crime/teen pregnancy/suicide/high dropout rates, and so on, to that of positive stories and innovations created by the *Latinnovators* I spotlight in this book. As my fellow author and friend Frank Carbajal likes to say, *"Es tiempo!"*—It's time!

I am hoping for something else too. I read a June 2010 *USA Today* article about a talented Latina in Chicago who wanted to go to college but whose father insisted that women belong at home. What I am hoping for is that this book, and the role models it contains, reaches those young people with immigrant parents who have never been to college in the United States. Those kids need guidance counselors on their side, not only encouraging them to go to college, but also guiding them through the many steps needed to apply, find funding, succeed academically and all the things that happen organically for kids in families where the parents have a college education.

Currently many of these kids are in schools with horrible counselor-to-student ratios. Many *never* get time with the counselor. These kids are left then under the influence of their uninformed, survival-minded parents telling them to just get a job after high school. Humberto's story demonstrates the cultural challenges that continue to exist in the Latino community vis-à-vis higher education. Until there are better college graduation rates for Latinos and a plethora of success stories *that reach these youth,* many will continue to believe they are not college material, that "people like us don't go to college." Many may even hear those words told directly to them by their parents and community, further discouraging them from aspiring to achieve a higher education. Robert and LA CAUSA are attacking that problem head on, but it needs to happen everywhere.

Have you seen the 2010 census data reports? Have you seen the explosive growth of America's Latino population in almost every state? By 2030, one of every two new entrants into the U.S. workforce will be Latino and one of every four Americans will be of Latino descent. By 2050, the U.S. Latino population is expected to reach 133 million, almost a full third of the U.S. population! [Source: Congressional Hispanic Caucus Institute] To return America to the #1 position globally in college degree attainment of its people, Latinos must earn 5.5 million college degrees by 2020. (Source: "The Roadmap for Ensuring America's Future," March 2011 report from Excelencia in Education.) This figure takes into account the projected population growth of Latinos in this time period and assigns a proportional number of the 36 million degrees that must be attained by all Americans, to the Latino community. That's an average of over 611,000 Latinos graduating from college each year. Factor in that 41% of American adult Latinos over the age of 20 don't have a regular high school diploma (Pew Hispanic Center report 5-13-2010) and that only 19% have earned an associate or higher degree, (2011 Excelencia report) and you start to see the economic crisis that's coming for our nation if drastic, large scale, real action isn't taken soon.

Current national, mostly negative, trends surrounding Latino youth and education (elementary, secondary and collegiate) *must* be reversed. It has become a national imperative directly tied to our country's economic future. Many are now focused on this effort, as evidenced by the sixty organizations that partnered with Excelencia for the study cited here.

The stories in this book are therefore instrumental. They show students successful people with similar backgrounds that escaped the community and familial negativity—or collective ignorance—about college, and instead chose the path of higher education. This is tremendously important to me—to get these stories in the hands of the most disadvantaged minority kids in our nation so that perhaps this way they can see that Mami and Papi's advice to start working after high school is wrong.

What have I learned as a result of this project? What revelations have I received by persevering for two years to make this book a reality?

In May of 2010, as I was writing this book, a humorous essay I penned was published in an anthology of UC Berkeley alumni writers. It's called "*When I was There: Life in Berkeley 1960-2010.*" Another essay in that same book helped me realize that something very important was happening to me as I wrote this book. Author Mary Pols wrote, "Never forget the privilege of being given a piece of somebody's life." Unlike the shorter interviews I did for the magazine article, this time I spent hours and hours with my interviewees. Each interview ranged from two to six hours. Mary's article showed me I was receiving incredible gifts from my subjects. It's funny, because they have been thanking me all along—for telling their stories, for immortalizing them and their achievements and for having the vision to write this book for the reasons I've written it. However, I am the one who must thank each of them—for the gift of giving me large pieces of their storied lives. It has indeed been a privilege for me. I feel humbled and honored for their trust in me to first listen to their stories and then to write them in a way that does justice to their lifetimes of achievement.

I gained new insights while doing this project that are worth sharing.

1. Many Latinos are culturally driven to conserve and reuse. Whether driven by poverty, wisdom of our grandparents, the social consciousness of our parents or perhaps all three, we are not people who waste much. We hold onto things until we can either reuse them or find a new home for them. I have learned I am not the only one who saves toilet paper rolls. We know the preschoolers will make binoculars, Christmas wreaths, mobiles, pirate scopes and other playthings with them once we donate them. I kept a bag of slightly stained clothes in my laundry room for years until I found someone that wanted to make a blanket with them. Meeting others around the country doing similar things somehow validates my otherwise odd behavior. I feel better now about giving up that precious square foot of space in my laundry room to keep something reusable out of the landfill. Now I know and respect where this tendency comes from, and I appreciate it. Many American families could learn a lot by observing how Latino families utilize things. We do it because it makes sense—it prolongs spending money to buy the next thing. We appreciate what we have and take nothing for granted.

2. Faith and fate make all things possible, if you actively participate in your own improvement. Having faith that things will improve is fine; it's what many of us were taught as young children in Latino homes. It is a belief rooted in our parents' religious values that have been passed on to my generation and now to our children. However, as I have told my mother my entire life, just having faith is not enough. You cannot just have faith that your life will improve and sit in your chair at home doing nothing else. Fate intervenes positively on behalf of those who have faith and are moving toward something. Frank Ramirez's story is ample proof of that. Having only faith would have assured his place at the steel mill and a life of labor there. Faith, *plus* his work to earn his Eagle Scout rank and his entering the local public speaking contest, set in motion the events that ultimately changed his life. Fate, in the form of a Scouting leader and a conversation 2,000 miles from home in a posh New York City hotel, made the difference.

3. Education never ends for the truly curious. While a strong proponent of formal education, I now realize that for many of us, education does not have a beginning and an end. We think of starting and ending formal educational programs. In reality, for the people you read about in this book and for our children, education is a spark we catch in our childhood that ignites over and over again in adulthood. For some the spark of education remains in one field: Humberto Rincon will always be an engineer and thank God for that! For others, myself included, there are different sparks that ignite, different interests to pursue, and new industries and fields to learn about. What if Frank Ramirez hadn't become curious about the energy requirements of data mining and processing? He would not have learned about the electrical grid status quo and pursued energy storage. One question led him to research something unknown to him, which yielded new discoveries. In science, this continuous asking of questions, of challenging the status quo, is commonplace. In business, not so much. In corporate settings, many tend to do what is expected—

to stay in their box and carry out the functional role they were hired to perform.

If we instead continuously educate ourselves about things that interest us along the way, we can become experts in two, three or four different things—and that is even better. Seeing how these leaders pursued new curiosities has also given me new perspective as a mother. Some parents push their children into a specific career path and begin doing so as early as preschool. I am taking a different path as a result of these stories. What I saw written on the wall of a children's museum is true: "The most important gift we can give to our children is the gift of curiosity." From now on, I will speak to audiences of young people about the curiosity they should develop as they pursue formal education, not about the need to pick a specific field and stick with it forever. That seems so 20th century. The 21st century curious mind chooses a field with which to start. It understands that in time, that field of knowledge may lead to other interests worth pursuing. The curious mind knows that pursing new knowledge is acceptable and encouraged. The curious and educated brain continues to evolve, expand, change directions and create new ideas based on interdisciplinary experiences. In that process, amazing things are imagined, and then created.

4. Sustainability is a frequently used yet rarely defined word that requires courage in action. One of my pet peeves has always been the use of buzz words and acronyms by people who do not understand their meaning. After interviewing twenty different entrepreneurs who have created sustainable businesses and organizations, here's my view of the word "sustainability". The process of:

• Questioning the industrial and social status quo

• Creating alternative solutions and processes to satisfy market and community needs

• To intentionally improve the environment and harm our planet less over time

For example, consider Sandra's story of seeing trash bins full of wasted fabric outside the fashion studio. She determined that practice was not sustainable or responsible. She took specific steps to create a business that rejects the status quo. Her creative reuse—giving throwaways a second, permanent life—directly benefits the environment.

True sustainability first requires the courage to question the status quo that is not sustainable. There are many places and practices that need someone to rise up and ask, "Why do we do it this way?" Master that ability and you too will be able to participate in the sustainability movement and create your own sustainable process, product or organization.

Without courage you will miss the chance to participate because you will be too passive and accepting of the status quo to affect any real change. Dennis Salazar's story is another example of the courage in action needed to reject the status quo mentality. You have seen what it takes to rethink an industry and to create and develop a truly green, sustainable business.

5. People frequently underestimate the power of personal and professional networks. One of the great personal growth experiences I had in researching and writing this book was growing my own network. When I started writing the article that ultimately inspired the book, I was working for a German communications firm that had been sold to a Los Angeles area billionaire running a private equity fund. My professional network was large and global. However, in looking back, it was limited to my military buddies, people in the communications industry and NSHMBA members in the San Francisco Bay Area. My network of women in business and my connections to the Latino business community were far smaller. As I transitioned out of my corporate role in the summer of 2009, I vowed to do a better job building up my network of fellow educated Latinos and Latinas. It was suddenly very important to me to do so—I felt like something had been missing from my life.

Writing that feature article gave me exactly the right starting point and I went with it. I tapped the network I had created through my years as a NSHMBA member. Those precious first NSHMBA contacts soon led me to a half dozen people to interview for the article. That number quickly doubled and I found myself picking and choosing who to interview based on what I could learn about them in advance. Truly lasting connections are made when you spend thirty minutes with someone going over the answers provided in the initial questionnaire, then two hours for a follow-up call, then four hours at the company facilities. As I left the offices of LA CAUSA on a sweltering July day in East Los Angeles, Robert Zardaneta said to me, "You will always have a home here. Come by anytime." The day after that, Carmen Rad sent an email to me thanking me for the visit to her downtown L.A. warehouse and offices. "I've realized that because you are writing this book, that our story will live on long after we have passed," she said. "Thank you for that."

When someone is generous enough to give you this much time because you're writing a book, you feel a tremendous sense of "WOW." I know these people will forever be part of my network and that I'll give back to them as much as they've given to me. If their kids want to know about flying for the Air Force, about attending UC Berkeley, about living in other countries, about global marketing best practices or what it's like working for a European conglomerate, they can call on me. I'll be there for them. Let this experience I'm sharing with you encourage you to not only build upon whatever networks you have in place, but to utilize them, to ask people in your network what they need and how you can help. The power of these connections is only obvious when you actively reach out and give.

6. The spirit of entrepreneurship can be sparked in one quick moment when decisive action is taken. As an entrepreneur myself, I have reaffirmed that just starting and moving forward is advantageous over hesitation and thinking too much about something. Carmen's story exemplifies that truth. Future entrepreneurs can also plan their sustainable business while working in a corporate setting gaining operational experience. When the time is right, the network is built, the customers identified and the plan in place, they can make the jump to entrepreneurship. Dennis Salazar's story demonstrates the value of this approach. The important lesson for entrepreneur "wannabes" is to realize there is not just one way to do it. Your intuition matters most in how you execute your plan to start your own business. If in doubt, just start!

7. Appreciate—and be encouraged by—the tendency toward entrepreneurship in the U.S. Latino community. The latest U.S. Census survey of businesses showed that growth of Hispanic-owned businesses was *double* the national average. In the U.S. Census survey before that one, Hispanic-owned businesses grew at *triple* the national average. The Census Bureau predicts that by 2012 there will be over three million Hispanic-owned businesses in the USA; 4.3 million just four years later. Did you know that there are almost 750,000 small businesses owned by Latinas? [Center for Women's Business Research] Why these tremendous growth rates? The simple answer, understood by anyone who has worked with socio-economically disadvantaged kids: given the opportunity to pursue a dream and demonstrate excellence, Latinos will jump on that opportunity and devote themselves completely. They will, like the millions of business owners represented in the Census data, work with every ounce of their being to persevere towards success, to create something of their own. The key is to be given the opportunity in the first place.

What's Next?

I encourage you to consider your educational and career paths and ask yourself if you will be contributing your talents to improving our environment or simply collecting a paycheck? Will you force your employer to look at sustainability initiatives seriously if he is not doing so already? Will you have the courage to take a stand against business practices that are not sustainable as the people in this book have done? If you are working somewhere that has a non-green printer or a non-green packaging company in the supply chain, will you suggest to your boss that they instead take a look at the approaches and innovations designed by Carmen Rad and Dennis Salazar? If you ask yourself and your friends these questions, you will likely gradually take steps to emulate the *Latinnovators* in this book. You will achieve professional success while honoring your environmental values through active advocacy. You too can become an environmental entrepreneur. This is why I'm speaking at universities and business schools. My contributions to the sustainability movement are two-fold. First, showcase today's environmental entrepreneurs and innovators for their courageous leadership and the path to get there. Second, encourage more soon-to-be graduates to emulate these educated big thinkers, with a special focus on encouraging young people within the Latino community.

If you are a Latina or Latino, please encourage your siblings, cousins and every high school and college student in your family to read this book. Our youth need to know that these role models and success stories exist, and that they are making an impact on our nation's economic future today. It pains me to hear that another Latina has "bitten the dust" by getting married right out of high school, for example. It pains me to hear her mother say, "Well, we don't have educated, successful Latinas around here that she could have met." Without visible role models and options, our kids are likely to make uninformed, short-term choices. This book can help focus them on the long term and provide insight into future possibilities for their lives.

This book can also help non-Latinos gain great insight. You can follow these career paths and find motivation from the moments when entrepreneurship was born within these leaders. You can benefit by understanding that in twenty years, one of every two people entering the U.S. workforce will be Latino. You will be more prepared than most to succeed in that new landscape because you will understand the aspirations and economic contributions of Latinos in this country.

I encourage parents to foster creative play and problem-solving in their children to form skillful engineers, talented designers or fearless entrepreneurs later in life. See the chapters about Humberto,

Sandra, and Carmen for examples of why creative play matters. I fear many parents unknowingly deprive their children of the intellectual foundation needed to innovate. You have read some fine examples of what creative play, reuse and problem-solving in childhood can result in during adulthood. If you are introducing video games to your kids while they are in preschool and elementary school as a way to fill the time, you are probably not encouraging creative play and problem-solving. Think about it.

Lastly, are you *latinnovating*? Or, do you know someone who is undertaking the task to make an existing business or industry more sustainable? Do you know someone who has created a business to improve the environment? If you answered yes to any of these questions, please visit the *Latinnovating* blog at www.blog. latinnovating.com and leave a comment telling me about yourself or the person you know. I have already begun to interview more entrepreneurs for the second book in the *Latinnovating* series. There are many more stories of leadership and entrepreneurship in this new economy that must be told and documented.

In fifty years, as America looks back to this point in time, to the beginning of the second decade of this century, I want it clearly documented that educated Latinos contributed significant intellectual and financial capital to making this nation more energy efficient and more environmentally responsible, while enjoying the fruits of their uniquely American dreams.

Additional Resources and Programs

Unified Communications Industry Recommended Reading

I lived and breathed unified communications for almost a decade. I continue to follow this industry. Here are some resources that will quickly get you up to speed on the unified communications industry, its players, its technologies and its success stories.

UCStrategies: This is the definitive place where analysts and consultants gather to write about new trends, technologies and implementation. Vendors post case studies here, and there is a daily news alert that keeps you informed on events and announcements around the industry. www.ucstrategies.com.

Gartner Magic Quadrant for Unified Communications: Gartner is one of the most respected technology analysis and consulting groups in the world. It influences many C-level enterprise decision makers who authorize the purchases of corporate systems. The group puts out *The Magic Quadrant for Unified Communications* report annually—it's like a "state of the union" view of the industry. The firm asks each vendor to put together extensive information about their product portfolio, their best customer success stories, their product roadmap, etc. Then the analysts rank and position the vendors in an easy-to-read grid.   www.gartner.com/technology/media-products/reprints/microsoft/vol10/article19/article19.html.

UCStrategies blog entry written by Marty Parker, long-time UC consultant: It's his commentary about the Gartner Magic Quadrant and a particularly good snapshot of where the industry is today www.ucstrategies.com/m_parker_Gartner_UC_MQ_2010. aspx?gnid=15383

Get Lean and Green Fast with Telecommuting: This is an industry white paper I helped co-author. It quantifies, in economic, carbon-reducing, and employee-retention terms, the green benefits of telecommuting and includes global examples of organizations using UC and collaboration technologies today. It includes many primary sources and research to help you understand and appreciate why more companies need to implement these remote working, eco-friendly initiatives. www.siemens-enterprise.com/main/Solutions/Green-Enter prise/~/media/AB774237D2634A298B2A127412052E73.pdf.

Unified Communications Magazine: This is a highly focused online publication with excellent guest bloggers and insight into trends. www.unified-communications.tmcnet.com.

Siemens Enterprise Communications: See how one established global UC vendor is demonstrating the green benefits of its technologies, reducing energy requirements, real estate requirements, equipment, and eliminating employee commuting. www.siemens-enterprise. com/us/about/green-enterprise.aspx

For All Girls

For young girls ages twelve through eighteen, I recommend attending an *Expanding Your Horizons in Science and Mathematics*™ conference. This event nurtures girls' interest in science and math courses to encourage them to consider careers in science, technology, engineering and math. It was started in 1974 as an informal group of women scientists and educators in the San Francisco Bay Area who were concerned about low female participation in math courses. I attended one of their conferences while in high school and it heavily influenced my decision to go to college. While flying for the military, I became heavily involved in planning EYH conferences in Washington

State and presented several aviation workshops. Visit this site to find an EYH conference near you. www.expandingyourhorizons.org

For Young Latinas

Latinitas Online Magazines: This non-profit organization is focused on informing, entertaining and inspiring young Latinas to grow into healthy, confident and successful adults. *Latinitas* Magazines are the first digital magazines made for and by Latina youth. Founded in 2002 in Austin, Texas as a project of Texas State University, their mission is to empower Latina youth through media and technology. www.latinitasmagazine.org

About the Author
Graciela Tiscareño-Sato

Graciela Tiscareño-Sato is the Founder and Chief Creative Officer of Gracefully Global Group LLC, a full service marketing and communications excellence firm, serving any organization needing original, compelling content to motivate an audience into action. This includes ghost blogging, ghost writing, book publishing and promotion services.

Before creating her own business, Graciela orchestrated and led various strategic and product marketing campaigns, including the Green Enterprise Initiative, at a Munich-headquartered communications software company. There she helped global enterprises understand the economic and sustainability benefits of collaboration technologies.

Graciela's years of experience as an out-in-front communicator make her highly effective in front of diverse types of audiences. Her public speaking career includes presenting to high school students, college students, business executives, educators and parents raising children with special needs. She is fully bilingual and an active mentor to Latino students. She holds an undergraduate degree from the University of California at Berkeley and completed her master's degree in international management at Whitworth College's School of Global Commerce during her active duty military career as an aviator with the United States Air Force.

Graciela was recognized by the Congressional Hispanic Caucus Institute (CHCI) seven months ahead of the publication of this book at the "Green Economy, Leading the Way" session of the 2010 CHCI Public Policy Conference. Graciela's thought-leadership pieces have been published in the United States and Europe, including in *Environmental Leader, Hispanic MBA, Communications News, Unified Communications, Enterprise Technology Management* and many others.

In May 2010, *LATINA Style Magazine* selected Graciela as "Entrepreneur of the Year" for the San Francisco area for "lifetime achievement and for being a visible role model to our young people." In November 2010, she was named "Entrepreneur of the Year" at the Anna Maria Arias Memorial Business Fund Dinner and Gala in Washington D.C. She is a key organizer of the annual Silicon Valley Latino Leadership Summit that brings together venture capitalists, entrepreneurs, executives and students to network and strategize in an intimate setting.

In addition to writing the next set of stories for *Latinnovating* Volume 2, Graciela is writing her military memoirs and will soon introduce her first children's book. The latter stars a Latina military aviator and her child. Graciela lives in the San Francisco East Bay with her husband and three inquisitive children who are well versed in recycling, composting, gardening, creative reuse and in-home energy efficiency. Contact Graciela via www.latinnovating.com.

Sato family photo

Graciela and her family on the University of California, Berkeley campus

Speeches and Services
Gracefully Global Group, LLC

Graciela Tiscareño-Sato is a frequent presenter at conferences, universities and association events. Her most in-demand presentation topics include:

Leadership

- "Leadership Lessons Learned from my Military Career: Applications in Business, Motherhood and Entrepreneurship." A unique content set that brings audiences specific, usable wisdom she learned while on active duty. Graciela shows how what was true back then in the cockpit is true today when raising children and running a business.

Latino-Led Innovation in the Green Economy

Created for high school students, college students, graduate business students and aspiring entrepreneurs, these presentations summarize the lessons and examples from this book and are tailored to each audience.

- "Latinos Shaping the Green Economy: How the Green Economy is Changing the World and How Latinos are Making a Difference"

- "Entrepreneurial Successes in the Green Economy: Role Models & Innovations from the Latino Community"

- "Latino-led Innovation in the Green Economy: Why it Matters"

- "Join the Women Leading the Green Economy"

- "Sustainability in Action: Ten Great Case Studies"

- "Inventing Your Own Green Career: Examples from Those Who Did it"

Professional Development and Personal Branding

This workshop was created for professionals already in the workforce who have accomplished fabulous things but who bore others when they talk about themselves.

- "You, the Brand"

Services

Graciela is a global marketing professional trained and experienced in all facets of the marketing discipline. To create new solutions, Graciela draws upon her unique life and professional experiences. These include two decades living and working on four continents, managing diverse work groups and fearless strategic thinking. Her global view and multicultural savvy, coupled with deep industry insight and connections, distinguish her creative processes.

Gracefully Global Group's mission is to create compelling content to inform, inspire and motivate people into action. Services include *all* aspects of original content creation and execution including:

- Ghost blogging (writing, editing and posting regular, relevant content from individuals or organizations)

- Ghost writing (memoirs, etc.)

- Publishing services (from editing to marketing plan to launch)

- Marketing messages (messages that motivate diverse business-to-consumer and business-to-business audiences)

- Strategic and product marketing plans (regional, national, global)

- Marketing collateral (datasheets, white papers, sales guides, etc.)

- Email and social media marketing campaigns

- Executive speeches for the press or analyst/consultant communities

- Multimedia customer success stories touting quantifiable benefits

Gracefully Global Group's publishing services are available to new and established authors. We are especially interested in bringing more success stories (and collections of stories) starring educated, accomplished Latinos out of the shadows and into the bright lights of America's mainstream media. *¡Es tiempo!* (It's time!) Contact us for guidelines to submit your book proposal and marketing plan. We can also, of course, develop a marketing plan for your book and assist in its execution.

In 2010, Gracefully Global Group LLC was named as the official marketing and communications firm for the Inaugural Silicon Valley Latino Leadership Summit. Together with author Frank Carbajal, founder of Es Tiempo LLC, and executive members of Hispanic-Net, Graciela is coordinating this annual summit to bring leaders in the private sector together with academics and public sector leaders, with a special focus on mixing entrepreneurs with venture capitalists and corporate executives. A key component of this event is bringing in talented high school and college students to connect them with potential mentors who are excellent examples of professional success and leadership. Attendees strategize and demonstrate actionable steps needed to ensure improved educational outcomes in the Latino community. They also create new business synergies while expanding their professional networks and take steps to elevate the profile of the Latino business community in the mainstream media.

Company-owned photo by Rob Baker

Graciela Tiscareño-Sato
Gracefully Global Group LLC

510·967·3339
grace@gracefullyglobal.com
www.gracefullyglobal.com

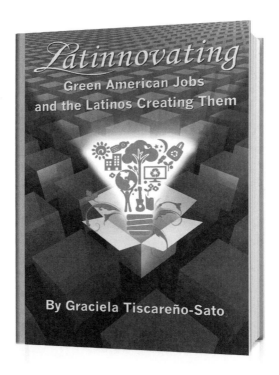

For more copies of *Latinnovating*, visit www.latinnovating.com. Trade, school and library buyers will find distributors listed under the Trade & Institutions tab on the website.

 Follow on Facebook. Search for Latinnovating.

 @Latinnovating
@GraceTiscareno

 www.linkedin.com/in/gracielatiscarenosato